Environmental Leadership
Equals
Essential Leadership

Environmental Leadership Equals Essential Leadership

Redefining Who Leads and How

John C. Gordon and Joyce K. Berry

with a foreword by Norman L. Christensen, Jr.

Yale University Press New Haven & London

Designed by James J. Johnson and set in Minion Roman type by Binghamton Valley Composition.
Tree illustration by Carol Marander.
Printed in the United States of America.

Library of Congress Cataloging-in-Publication Data

Gordon, J. C. (John C.), 1939–
    Environmental leadership equals essential leadership : redefining who leads and how / John C. Gordon and Joyce K. Berry.
        p. cm.
    Includes bibliographical references and index.
    ISBN-13: 978-0-300-10891-0 (alk. paper)
    ISBN-10: 0-300-10891-5 (alk. paper)

    1. Environmental responsibility—Study and teaching (Higher)—United States.   2. Conservation leadership—Study and teaching (Higher)—United States.   3. Leadership—Study and teaching (Higher)—United States.   I. Berry, Joyce K.   II. Title.
GE195.7.G67 2006
333.72'0684—dc22

                                                                2005023924

A catalogue record for this book is available from the British Library.

The paper in this book meets the guidelines for permanence and durability of the Committee on Production Guidelines for Book Longevity of the Council on Library Resources.

10   9   8   7   6   5   4   3   2   1

Contents

Foreword

Environmental Leadership Indeed!

Fifteen years ago, I was asked to lead a new enterprise at Duke University, an entity we had the chutzpah to call a "School of the Environment." The expectation of the university's trustees was that this school would become a world leader in "education, research, and service to understand basic environmental processes and to protect and enhance the environment and its natural resources for future generations." Like so many would-be leaders, especially in academe, I was selected to lead for reasons that were largely unrelated to the challenges I would face. I had been a pretty reasonable teacher and scholar and had said yes often (too often, perhaps) to requests for help with administrative needs. With equal and large measures of hubris and naïveté, I agreed to lead what would eventually become the Nicholas School of the Environment and Earth Sciences.

Over the next decade, I learned the art and craft of environmental leadership from numerous sources, including lots of mistakes, several patient mentors, and many excellent role models (among them, the authors of this book). I would have loved to have owned this volume when I started that journey.

So, what is so different about *environmental* leadership that it should be distinguished from leadership in other areas? Much of this volume is dedicated to this question. Early in my deanship, I discovered how important clear answers to this question were, as I worked to build a sense of community among faculty, staff, and students, and a sense of commitment and stewardship from the senior university administration and financial supporters. From my perspective, there are four ingredients: boundaries, priorities, uncertainties, and action.

Among the most interesting and daunting characteristics of environmental issues is the extent to which they permeate virtually all *boundaries.* Ecologists remind us constantly that ecosystems, at whatever scale we choose to study or manage them, are open to the movement of matter and energy both in and out. Actions in upland forests directly influence processes in wetlands that, in turn, alter the behavior of aquatic and marine ecosystems. Today's global economies and communication systems ensure that information and human values that affect the ecosystems on which we depend are transmitted instantaneously with little regard for the boundaries of nations and regional alliances. For example, decisions to cut or not cut forests in one region have an immediate effect on the nature of forest management in other regions, because of effects on global wood fiber markets. Because of a willingness to contribute to the efforts of a welter of environmental organizations, people who may never actually visit the Amazon or the Arctic National Wildlife Refuge have a substantial say in their future management.

Arbitrary jurisdictional and institutional boundaries relative to environmental processes and problems present truly significant challenges. Consider how often counties, states, and nations are separated by rivers that literally cut watersheds in half and generate conflict over responsibility for managing both water quantity and quality. The three-, twelve-, or two-hundred-mile boundaries that define national jurisdictions in marine waters have little relationship to the movement of ocean waters or the resources they contain. Jurisdictional fragmentation of responsibility among government agencies creates additional boundaries and management challenges that are exemplified by the many federal agencies whose actions influence the future of stocks of migratory fish such as salmon.

The solutions to environmental problems (whether climate change, species conservation, or water quality management) demand communication, understanding, and collaboration among diverse disciplines and traditions. The problem solving requires an understanding of basic science-based processes, the roles of humans as problem causers and solvers, and the potential health, engineering, and organizational management options that might be applied to a problem. Centuries of increasing specialization and trends toward decentralized management of schools and departments have done little to prepare the academic world to meet environmental challenges that defy traditional academic boundaries.

It is tempting for some to see the boundary challenge as a need for redesign. We would manage better if we could simply redraw geographic boundaries, redefine the jurisdiction of agencies, redesign curricula, or define new disciplines and departments. Many of the boundaries I have just described serve important functions, even if they present challenges to environmental problem solving. But within the vast domain of environmental issues, the sobering truth is that boundaries useful for the solution of one problem are likely to be quite unsuitable for another.

John Gordon and Joyce Berry argue convincingly that the antidote to the boundary problem is problem-oriented, systems-based thinking. Effective environmental leaders assess the extent of a challenge by the spatial and temporal scale of physical and biological processes that drive it, as well as its cultural, social, and institutional dimensions. Rather than trying to destroy or redefine boundaries, they then look for strategies to mitigate them or work across them.

The litany of environmental challenges appears to be limitless, but the resources we can muster to meet those challenges are painfully limited. Thus, leaders must be able to set clear *priorities* among a gaggle of competing needs and demands. Newly anointed leaders are often surprised to discover just how sparse the priority-setting toolbox is.

In the midst of competing demands, the most worrisome temptation for leaders is to yield to the loudest or most recent voice. Nearly as worrisome are the pressures to go for the "low-hanging fruit" and set priorities based on easiness or low cost. As John Gordon and Joyce Berry emphasize throughout this book, decision making based on these sorts of criteria is the antithesis of essential leadership. They point out that given the emotional atmosphere in which environmental decisions often must be made, conflict resolution and negotiation skills are critical leadership attributes. But good leaders also recognize that resolution of conflict may not by itself be a particularly worthy way to set priorities. When conflict rises to the level of chaos or violence, priority setting is difficult indeed. However, civil argument and dispute often clarifies decision choices and the values that underpin them. Furthermore, priority setting overly focused on minimizing conflict runs the serious risk of producing less-than-ideal solutions.

Many times I have wished for an objective decision tool, such as a computer program into which I could feed my dilemma and all the relevant data and out of which would come a rational prioritization. In this regard, much has been written and said about the power of risk-based cost-benefit analysis. There are compelling arguments in favor of the view that decisions should be informed by an objective (quantitative, if possible) assessment of the likelihood and consequences of particular actions compared to an assessment of their costs. Note that I said "informed by" and not "based on."

There are many ways to calculate risks, and selecting from among them often involves value-laden choices. For example, one might choose to express the risk of an environmental threat in terms of lives lost or life-years lost. That choice depends entirely on the value one places on the lives of younger versus older people. To complicate things further, ameliorating one risk nearly always involves tradeoffs with other risks, as in the current debate over the use of DDT (for example, the tradeoff between its impacts on ecosystems and its effectiveness in combating mosquito-borne disease).

All these issues emphasize one of the central themes in this book: vision and values are the most basic leadership tools.

Uncertainty is a major challenge to leadership in many endeavors, but most especially in matters related to the environment. Such uncertainty arises from three sources—ignorance, variability, and complexity—and understanding the source matters to leaders.

If I knew more, I could lead more effectively. Our ignorance of the elements of ecosystems and the social systems that interact with them is profound, yet in some ways this is the easiest sort of uncertainty with which to cope. It is the rationale for much environmental research. The central challenge presented here is, in the midst of many unknowns, to direct research toward those unknowns that are most critical to leadership decisions.

By variability, I refer to our ability to often predict the

average character or behavior of collections of things, but those predictions become shaky as we focus on individual examples. This is, of course, a statistical problem, and we can narrow the range of this uncertainty by expanding our monitoring and increasing our sample sizes. More important, effective leaders understand that understanding this sort of variability is critical to setting expectations for the likely range of outcomes from specific decisions.

Ecosystems and social systems are incredibly complex! On the surface, this statement seems about as useful as Douglas Adams's assertion in *The Hitchhiker's Guide to the Galaxy* that "The Universe is a really big place!" Small, undetectable, and, therefore, unmanageable variations in the state of system components can produce enormously different results. If ignorance defines the limits of what we know, chaos defines the limits of what we *can* know. From a practical standpoint, this means that surprises are inevitable, and essential leadership cannot be in denial on this point.

Environmental change is ubiquitous and inexorable. Given this truth, inaction often has potent consequences; the decision to do nothing is often followed by a torrent of change. Thus, it is not too much to argue that effective environmental leadership must embrace what the corporate world has come to call "change management." Essential leaders do not just acknowledge change as inevitable but strive to find in it new opportunity.

The connection between leadership and *action* is explicit and implicit throughout this book. The temptation not to act derives from laziness, bewilderment, and/or the perception of impotence. We can dispense with laziness right away; "lazy leadership" is a true oxymoron, although lazy individuals will often blame their inaction on powerlessness or uncertainty.

Uncertainty is often said to lead to "analysis paralysis." In the words of Kai N. Lee, "Learning is valuable, but it is always a precarious value compared to action." Nearly two decades ago, I took part in a review of the science underpinning management in a federal natural resource agency. The tagline for our report read "You can't manage what you don't understand." Years later, given the inevitable and immense uncertainties associated with environmental challenges, my response to this assertion is, "The hell you can't."

The daunting truth is that environmental leaders must constantly act in the context of uncertainty and change. As John Gordon and Joyce Berry suggest, essential leadership ensures that such management is truly adaptive to new knowledge and changing conditions. Successful adaptive management depends on clearly stated operational goals as well as models that connect actions to outcomes. Most important, leadership is undertaken with a humility that assumes that the models or maybe even the goals are incorrect, and it is therefore willing to undertake and learn from monitoring programs that honestly measure management success.

Often with justification, constituencies are skeptical of adaptive management programs; "you mean you don't know what you're doing?" Successful adaptive leadership ultimately depends on the ability to earn the trust of followers and stakeholders. They must have confidence that leaders will accept and respond to new understanding and that leaders will foster cultures that do the same.

Above all else, essential leaders believe that their actions, large or small, will matter. Successful leaders subscribe to British philosopher Edmund Burke's admonition that "nobody made a greater mistake than he who did nothing because he could do only a little." More than that, they are able to convey that same spirit to those they lead.

Returning to a question posed earlier, "What is so different about *environmental* leadership that it should be distinguished from leadership in other areas?" Boundaries, priorities, uncertainty, and action are indeed challenges to many endeavors. But in few areas do these issues converge so persistently as with the environment.

Gordon and Berry eschew what they call "leadership inflation," the tendency for leadership volumes to showcase giants on the world stage. Instead, they focus their attention on what they call "essential" leadership, that is, the sort of leadership that is likely to engage each of us on an everyday basis. They make a splendid case for their central assertion that "environmental leadership consists largely of learned skills and styles and that learning needs to begin early and last a lifetime," and they provide a wonderfully compact and concise guide for that journey.

Norman L. Christensen, Jr.
Professor and Founding Dean
Nicholas School of the Environment and
Earth Sciences
Duke University

Preface: Why This Book?

There are lots of books on leadership. Why should there be another, especially this one? Why "essential" leadership and not just leadership? Our answers to these questions are linked, and require a brief history of our leadership experience, which has been academic and entrepreneurial.

As academics, we have taught leadership courses to graduate and undergraduate students for over a decade at the Yale School of Forestry and Environmental Studies and the Colorado State University College of Natural Resources. We have also taught leadership in executive education settings such as Yale's Corporate Environmental Leadership Seminar (CELS), the Council of State Governments, environmental and nonprofit organizations, and in international settings, including the United Nations Development Programme. Our students in these courses have been mostly people working and studying in wildlife and conservation biology, forestry, environmental health and safety, industrial ecology, and natural resource management. They have come from and gone on to a huge variety of organizations, including multinational corporations, nongovernmental organizations, and consulting firms; and an array of federal, state, and local government agencies ranging from the Central Intelligence Agency to state fish and game management organizations. We have experienced entrepreneurial leadership, having started a consulting firm and a sustainable forestry business. We have participated in and led integrated assessments on a variety of problems and for a variety of organizations, ranging from the National Park Service to the Intertribal Timber Council and the International Paper Company. In both our academic and other roles, we have "met payrolls"; hired and fired; delighted and infuriated employees, clients, and the general public; seen our leadership lauded and criticized; and generally run the gamut of ordinary leadership experience. Our point is not that we think our experience is particularly exceptional and exemplary, and thus to be followed. Precisely because our experience is ordinary and we have learned from it, we think there are many people like us who can benefit from what we have learned.

In the face of our variety of experience, we were at first surprised and then gratified to find a set of strong common themes in the ways that environmental leaders and students think and behave. These themes form the backbone of this book. Effective people in environmental jobs tend to have a common set of views about problem solving, about ethics, and about those characteristics that are most important for effective organizational leadership.

Our own experience is foremost in academic leadership, and one of our findings is that academic experience is good training for essential leadership generally. Most academic leadership posts are filled with those who have made their mark as researchers and teachers. They rarely have any formal management or leadership training, and thus have to learn to lead on the job, quickly, or fail. We discovered personally we could learn to lead. An aid in this is that universities are short on "command-and-control" situations. Academic leaders, perhaps even more so than those in industry and government, must be adept at getting strong individuals to do what is good for the whole organization without being able to force or order them to do so.

Thus, we use our own experience (as well as the reported experience of others) to illustrate major themes in environmental leadership. Because we now believe that all modern leadership in all organizations is taking on the characteristics we observed in environmental ones, we use the term *essential leadership* to indicate this broadening of application. "Essential" in this use refers to the fact that the themes describe the essence, the core, of modern leadership and that effective leadership makes understanding these themes necessary for modern leaders.

In addition to our experience, we have based this book on a new survey of selected leaders. We chose leaders from a broad and deep experience base, and their answers to our questions illustrate many of our own observations about the nature of essential leadership.

Finally, we stress "ordinary" experience because we think there is a negative principle that we call "leadership inflation" at work in the study and literature of leadership. We all can and should try to learn from Confucius, Lincoln, Churchill, and the legion of politicians and heads of companies that are so thoroughly examined in leadership books. But how similar are your life and your challenges likely to be to theirs? Perhaps "real-world, day-to-day" situations and people are more valuable objects for practical study for most of us. Probably, for example, running a modest-sized nonprofit organization, or a division of a major company, is not much like leading a large nation through a war.

Ten years ago, our first leadership text, *Environmental Leadership: Developing Effective Skills and Styles,* brought together our experience with that of a variety of environmental leaders. Their reported experience and our conclusions from it remain valid today. But much has changed in the world. Globalization of the world economy, the collapse of the Soviet Union, the rise of China as an economic power, the tragedy of 9/11 and the "war on terror," the rise of the Internet, better understanding of and greater concern about such environmental threats as global warming and invasive species, the inflation and collapse of a worldwide stock market bubble, and market-driven certification of agricultural and forest practices and products are just some of the major changes in the world since our first book. The context for leadership has changed.

In this book we translate our experience and the results of our leadership survey into a tool for continuously learning leadership in this relatively new century. On completing the book, a reader will have a good grasp of what we think essential leadership is, why it is different in some major ways from "old" leadership, and how to both learn it as an individual and install and use it in an organization.

Acknowledgments

We wish to thank the respondents to the survey included in this book; the authors of our previous book; those who reviewed this book; the students in our courses who shaped our thinking; Joyce Ippolito, manuscript editor; Carol Marander, graphic illustrator at Colorado State University; and our hardworking editor, Jean Thomson Black. The following presses and authors kindly gave us permission to use portions of their work:

Berrett-Koehler Publishers	Island Press
Leslie Carothers	Ronald Pellman
Jim Collins	Carol Rosenblum Perry
James Crowfoot	Gifford Pinchot
Louis V. Gerstner, Jr.	Jeff Sirmon
Rudolph W. Giuliani	Jack Ward Thomas
HarperCollins Publishers	Henry H. Webster
Hyperion	

Chapter 1

Becoming an Essential Leader

Environmental problems have characteristics that make them particularly hard to solve, and we define environmental leaders as people who are capable of solving environmental problems. As world population increases, so does the demand on natural and human resources. Increased human need coupled with the increased ability to travel and communicate make problems more complex. For example, the consumption of paper still increases in lock step with the number of people in the world. Most of the raw material for paper comes from forests, and forests provide many benefits to people other than paper.

Thus arguments arise about the use of forests, arguments that cannot be resolved "scientifically" without knowledge of forests that is not yet available. Strong emotions often emerge in discussions of forests. At the Seventh American Forest Congress, which in 1996 brought together a wide variety of people to talk about the future of forests in the United States, over 10 percent of the participants thought that physical violence was an appropriate way to resolve some conflicts over forest use. This narrow illustration contains the ingredients that make most environmental problems "wicked" ones: long times to solutions, complex interactions of components and people, a weak and scattered science base, a need for integration across disciplines to understand or solve them, and an atmosphere that is emotion-charged and contentious. When all of these five characteristics are taken together they imply a sixth: the likelihood of surprises and unintended consequences born of uncertainty.

In our view, all important problems that leaders confront increasingly take on these characteristics, and are calling forth the same leadership skills and styles that we described in our earlier book, *Environmental Leadership:*

Developing Effective Skills and Styles. To reflect this broadening, we now call the leadership we describe here "essential leadership," to reflect the changes in the essence, the core skills and styles, of leadership, and to indicate that successful leadership necessarily incorporates them. All complex problems involve tradeoffs among the values of those who have the problem and those who seek its solution. For example, landfills have to go somewhere, and people in their vicinity feel their presence more than people far away do. Essential leaders are good at confronting this sort of complexity and at dealing with uncertainty. Henry Webster (1993, 105) described environmental leaders as absorbers of uncertainty who lead in complex situations through "thinking and co-operation." Ethics, a secure and clear knowledge of right and wrong and how to apply it, are a major and tricky component of leadership under uncertainty. Essential leaders have to be exceptionally sensitive to the values of all those with a stake in their decisions and actions. At the same time, they have to be exceptionally good at separating their own personal values from those of their clients and those for whom their solutions have major effects. Often, the claim is made

3

that regard for the environment contains a special kind of ethics, such as the "land ethic" proposed by Aldo Leopold. In so far as this is true, environmental leadership implies a broader ethical base that includes "nature" as well as humans. But ethical behavior, perhaps particularly in environmental management, requires not only, or even primarily, that you be good at seeing a lack of proper behavior in others, but rather that you constantly review your own behavior with respect to the values of others. This is difficult because environmental people often truly want to save the world from perceived environmental evils that have become the basis for much of their personal value system. A major component of environmental, and increasingly all, leadership is to be able to practically reconcile strong personal values with the different values of others whom the leader serves.

It is particularly from leading attempts to answer questions arising outside science using data, methods, and people from inside science ("integrated, science-based assessments") that we have formed the view that all leadership tends toward the methods and skills that are particularly important in environmental leadership. Communication across the formidable barrier that separates science from the rest of the world is always difficult. In general communication technology has made information, including scientific information, more accessible to all, and to many more than just a few years ago. But this very surfeit of information can make communication more difficult and complex, for example when a subject is described without reference to the sampling or methodological limitations on the description. Similarly, the rise of market capitalism and democracy has given many more people the notion they are stakeholders in activities that previously seemed remote or unimportant. Most people feel they can or should influence policy with their vote, and be able to vote with their money in the marketplace. Leaders no longer have as great an edge in information or influence as they once had. At the same time, the multiplication of technical specialties has spread responsibility for solving specific problems within and among a great variety of people and organizations. These trends mean that leadership has a greater component of persuasion and inclusiveness than in the past, and that problem solving requires a higher order of synthesis than in the past.

Another relevant observation makes all leadership directly related to environmental leadership. As communication and science make the global commons better known to all, it is increasingly clear that all humans share the same environment (in addition, as Lily Tomlin has said, "time-sharing the same atoms") and are at the same time an increasingly influential component of what we call "nature" (McKibben 1990). No place or component of the biosphere is completely uninfluenced by human activity. In most places, most of the time, human activity dominates. All human activity can be seen as environmentally based and important to the future of the envelope that contains humanity. Every human activity thus has an environmental dimension and all leadership decisions and actions become in some significant measure "environmental."

In *Environmental Leadership: Developing Effective Skills and Styles* we selected leaders from a variety of organizations and backgrounds to give their views on a particular leadership skill or organizational leadership style. From these authors and from the leadership literature and our own experience we formed a set of hypotheses about environmental leadership and environmental problem solving. The most important of these are:

- Leadership is a set of skills that can be learned (leaders are made not born).
- Everyone needs to learn to lead and follow as circumstances dictate.
- Problem solving is the central leadership skill.
- Leaders must think positively and continually about change.
- Breadth and flexibility need to be cultivated to cope with complexity.
- Listening is the central leadership communication skill.
- Successful leaders operate from a strong ethical base.
- Continual, "lifelong" learning allows leaders to grow and change with the times.

These hypotheses formed this book in two major ways. First, we took these hypotheses out as survey questions to a set of contemporary leaders that included but went beyond the set of leaders who were authors for our first book. We particularly wanted to see leadership in the context of social trends, through the eyes of experienced environmental leaders. For the survey we defined environmental leaders as people who had a leading role in an organization that had to solve or help solve environmental problems. We drew respondents from private for-profit and not-for-profit organizations, and from government and academia.

The "leadership tree" concept is the second way the hypotheses informed this book (Figure 1). We think a tree is a good analogy for the way the elements of essential leadership are integrated. The roots represent the core values and ethical system particular to each individual student of leadership. Similarly, the trunk represents the skills and styles that each individual possesses. The branches and leaves are the application of the values and skills to problems and relationships necessary to solve them, and the fruit represents accomplished solutions and fruitful relationships. We use the tree in two ways as a leadership learning tool. First, we encourage you to use the tree concept to carefully inventory your values, skills, and experience in solving problems. Once the inventory is complete, you will be able to identify areas for concentrated learning and create a leadership learning plan. Your leadership learning plan, ideally a carefully written and reviewed document, includes:

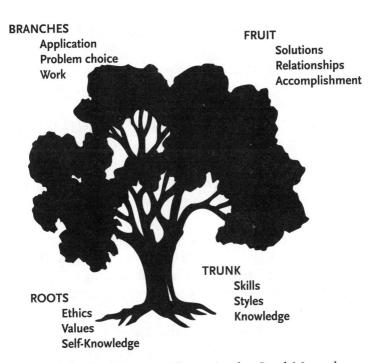

BRANCHES
 Application
 Problem choice
 Work

FRUIT
 Solutions
 Relationships
 Accomplishment

TRUNK
 Skills
 Styles
 Knowledge

ROOTS
 Ethics
 Values
 Self-Knowledge

FIG. 1. **A leadership tree.** (Illustration by Carol Marander, Colorado State University)

- Your leadership tree elements: self-knowledge, values, ethics; leadership skills and styles; self and skills applied to problems; and leadership accomplishments, including solved problems.

- A description of a leadership learning group: those people with whom you can share leadership experiences and from whom you can get honest review and feedback.

- A list of your leadership characteristics, including those you regard as strengths and those that need the most work (see Chapter 3).

- Your "leaders to watch" list: those individuals from whom you think you can learn, either in person or remotely, as through the Internet or other media.

- Your personalized leadership reading list; add summaries and lessons as you read to create your own leadership text.

- Your schedule of leadership learning activities, including meetings with your leadership group, work on leadership skills and styles you need to polish, opportunities to observe and talk with leaders, and your reading tasks.

- Your monitoring and mentoring plan: how you will track your development as a leader and with whom you will check your progress.

Essentials

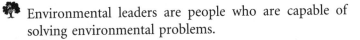 Environmental leaders are people who are capable of solving environmental problems.

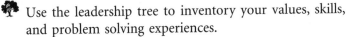 The six defining characteristics of environmental problems:

> Long times to solution
> Complexity
> Weak and scattered science base
> Integration across disciplines
> Emotionally charged atmosphere
> Uncertainty and unintended consequences

 Environmental characteristics have become essential for all kinds of leadership and therefore we call new leadership "essential leadership."

 Essential leadership can be learned, and problem solving is the central leadership skill.

Use the leadership tree to inventory your values, skills, and problem solving experiences.

 Create your own personal leadership plan to identify leadership learning opportunities and actions.

Chapter 2

Leaders See Today's World

In our first book, *Environmental Leadership: Developing Effective Skills and Styles,* we asked environmental leaders to contribute chapters describing their own personal leadership path and the skills and styles they believed were most important for today's leaders. Nine years later, we returned to these chapter authors, as well as other environmental leaders, and asked them to respond to a questionnaire about leaders and leadership in the twenty-first century.

The purpose of the questionnaire was to reexamine the lessons learned from *Environmental Leadership* and to provide a broader social context for environmental leadership. For instance, collaborative leadership styles were "front and center" in the 1990s. The model of an authoritarian, hierarchical leader who identified organizational goals and infused them from the top down was replaced by the leader who worked in a participatory team environment where goals were created in a collaborative and shared decision-making process. The decade of the 1990s was also a time when many believed that men and women displayed different leadership skills and styles; for example, some believed women demonstrated better listening skills than men, or men focused more on product and action rather than process.

Our questionnaire thus was based on what we believed were the most common current ideas about leadership. We began by identifying a total of seventy environmental leaders in the private, public, and nonprofit sectors. We received thirty completed surveys (we list respondents in the Appendix) representing 600-plus years of total leadership experience.

The first five survey questions were open ended and

asked each leader's perspective on (1) important social trends or conditions affecting today's environmental leaders, (2) major barriers facing today's leaders, (3) how leaders emerge in their individual organizations, and (4) what five characteristics they think most important for today's leaders. The next section listed twelve statements about leadership and asked for a response from "strongly agree" to "strongly disagree." We then asked respondents to describe a location where they had observed effective leadership and to describe a situation where leadership was needed but missing. The purpose of these two questions was to transfer leadership skills and styles from the hypothetical to the real world. Our view has always been that the best way to learn leadership is from real leaders and leadership situations. The final two questions asked for the advice respondents would give to future environmental leaders, and for any last thoughts or comments.

Thanks to the wisdom and experiences of these environmental leaders, we were able to gather a wealth of information. This chapter discusses important social trends and major barriers facing today's leaders and provides insights through direct quotes from our respondents, as well as characteristics and styles they thought important to future environmental leadership.

The views of environmental leaders are a clear reflection of the fundamental societal changes occurring in the United States and worldwide in the first decade of the twenty-first century. Globalization, population, and demographic changes; shifts in public values and ethics; the role of government, economic, and social policy; the technological revolution and environmental complexity; and education all are identified by the majority of our respondents as creating the context for leadership.

Almost every leader highlighted the influence of globalization and the polarizing issues between poor and rich countries. One leader noted three world conditions where the first two "worlds" of developed (the United States, Europe, and Japan) and less-developed (Asia and Latin America) countries are leaving developing countries such as those in sub-Saharan Africa behind and in desperate condition. The globalization of capital and the decrease in trade barriers indicate to some that more pressure will be put on developing countries to produce the resources that Americans desire but are increasingly unwilling to produce from their own resource base. A growing worldwide population also creates a situation where scarce resources are stressed by human demand and encroachment into natural areas. In 2002 the conflict created by the needs of rich and poor countries and the impacts of a global economy were at the forefront of the second Global Summit on Sustainable Development. Whereas the first Environmental Summit in Rio (1991) focused on biodiversity, global warming, and forestry initiatives, the difficult issues of rich versus poor were much more at the forefront of the second Summit, illustrating that the environment is no longer an isolated issue but at the heart of our global future. As one respondent said, "It will be increasingly difficult to ask people who are struggling to find food and water today to set aside resources to serve tomorrow."

For most of American history, natural resources were viewed as products necessary to build communities and support a growing, expanding population, similar to the current situation of many developing countries. The shift to a more protectionist view of natural resources and the environment began slowly in the United States in the 1960s with the Wilderness Act, the National Environmental Policy Act, and then accelerated in the 1970s with legislation such as Clean Air and Clean Water Acts, the Endangered Species Act, and the National Forest Management Act. For many, Earth Day 1970 became the icon of the environmental awakening of the American public. In the late 1980s, fires in Yellowstone National Park, oil spills in Alaska, pollution on the beaches of the west and east coasts, and fears of global warming and diminishing open space brought environmental issues to the front door of average Americans. The public began to realize that the environment and natural resources were not just some faraway pristine places but were influencing their daily lives. By 1993, President Clinton had convened the first Forest Summit in Portland, Oregon, to overcome what was often called natural resources policy "gridlock" in the Pacific Northwest. Fierce disagreements over protection of northern spotted owl habitat in old-growth forests and timber harvesting symbolized the deep polarization of values between people committed to either "owls" or "jobs." Today, leaders encounter diverse and environmentally concerned publics who want to have a voice in environmental matters of all kinds. In our survey responses, leaders point to a continuing clash of values and contentious environments in which "ego-centered self-interests impede forming common good consensus."

Environmental leaders note that the shift in environmental values is compounded by an increasingly urbanized and mobile population that has no experience with, and little knowledge of, natural places and resources. People feel disconnected from the land and have a diminished sense of place. One leader expressed concern about the "inherent difficulty of educating an increasingly disenfranchised and unprepared public about very complex issues." Others pointed to the maturity of baby boomers with wealth and time on their hands that has created a "me" society where people are less willing to sacrifice current comfort for future goals, including environmental ones. Overall, leaders describe a "disconnect between environmental values and personal lifestyles where consumers are willing to pay more for products but not willing to reduce their consumption." Regardless of cause, the reality is that today's leaders will encounter diverse and vocal publics with strongly held values about natural resources, who first and foremost have protection of their own environment on their minds.

Access to information and the complexity of environmental issues appear often in our leaders' picture of the twenty-first century. Communications today are "fast and pervasive; information is no longer power" writes one. The USDA Forest Service demonstrated the power and role of the Internet in the twenty-first century by using it to provide information and gather public input about Clinton's controversial roadless area policy. Citizens today can use their own computers to look at natural resource maps derived from geographic information systems, and create their own management schemes for a particular area. Leaders also mentioned the role of the media when identifying important social trends, often expressing the prevalence of "sensational journalism and the emphasis on headlines versus substance."

The complexity of today's environmental issues creates additional challenges for environmental leaders. Survey respondents wrote of the "sheer complexity" of issues, some that are "too complex to resolve successfully," as well as there being "less respect for the scientific method." Others note the success of technological developments "to help solve what were once thought of as intractable problems such as genetic engineering to ease famine and forestry land use." Complexity appears to be a defining feature of environmental leadership in an era when emphasis is placed on large landscapes and ecosystems as well as on the integration of sustainable human and natural communities. In this era of complexity, leaders frequently mention *the need for the integration of essential sciences, and in forms that can be comprehended by the public and decision makers.*

Focusing on government, leaders identified an "anti-government sentiment" and general "lack of confidence in government to set goals and make decisions." Leaders point to the "increasing role of the states, blurring of public and private sectors, and deregulation and privatization" as key factors influencing the role of government. As a result of the general distrust of government, policy formation and delivery are filled with challenge. One said, "The clear message is about a multiplicity of strident and diverse interest groups" who "utilize the system to pursue their own goals." Another said, "It is a muddled period where true courage must be exercised by the few leaders that may exist because they will not get much clear support for issues that are almost without direction today." One leader notes, "the 'environment' is one of those politically correct issues that everyone is definitely for, but few have the stomach to propose the really tough, long-term solutions." It is this sense of frustration that sparked the Seventh American Forest Congress and calls for a new way of doing the nation's environment and natural resource business. Community-based stewardship groups and ecosystem management partnerships also began to emerge in the mid-1990s as new models of collaborative, and often science-based, decision making.

The overall picture of current social trends and conditions described by leaders was one of a contentious and resource-consuming American public that has increasing access to information but is generally not well educated about the complexity of environmental issues and continues to show little confidence in government. This provides the background for one leader's view that "finding, training, encouraging, mentoring, and supporting the next generation of leaders is the greatest challenge for today's leaders."

We developed a number of survey questions to help us confirm or reevaluate today's most important leadership skills, styles, and characteristics based on many of the lessons learned and insights gleaned from preparing our first book. First we asked respondents, "For the most part, do today's leaders need different skills/styles than past leaders?" Twenty-five said yes, and five replied no. For those who said yes, the box lists those skills and styles they identified.

In addition, we asked leaders, "What five characteristics do you think are the most important for today's leaders?" Similar to our findings in *Environmental Leadership,* communication and listening skills topped the list, closely followed by interpersonal skills. Through our personal interviews and other surveys over the past fifteen years, we have been consistently told that environment and natural resource leaders have a good understanding of biological and ecosystem sciences, but the greatest educational need is for much

New leadership skills and styles identified by survey respondents.

- Real understanding of major societal needs and ability to clearly articulate how resource management links to these needs.
- Team approach.
- Ability to communicate and work with a much wider range of stakeholder interests.
- Ability to observe and understand the dynamics of individual groups.
- Today's leaders lead at the will of those led.
- International leadership effectiveness.
- Broad base of knowledge.
- Past leaders were much more autocratic, motivated through fear and power.
- Proactive problem solving.
- To be a leader you have to take chances and stand out.
- Today's leaders need excellent relationship building skills to get things done. They cannot "force" a decision and make it stick.
- More adaptable to change; ability to value different cultures.

- Action must replace inaction.
- No one person can "run" anything of any significant size any more and "be the boss." We have to be prepared to stand back and let different people with different kinds of skills step forward to contribute their part when called for.
- Problems are more complex. More need for thoughtfulness and adaptability.
- Communication and persuasive skills are in higher demand than ever.
- A major task of today's leaders is not only to build and lead their organization successfully, but in addition, they must get their vision out to the public.

greater understanding of public values and effective public involvement processes. Again in 2001, survey respondents advised that leaders must be "as interested in the human relations aspects of issues as the technical." They need to "be open to new ideas and cultures," "build relationships," and "find common ground." Personal integrity is also high on leaders' lists of characteristics. Given the complexity of environmental problems, leaders emphasized that critical skills include the ability to "deal with uncertainty and change, vision, flexibility, and risk taking." Leaders, they said, also must be "integrated thinkers, politically savvy and with the guts to make decisions."

Some may feel intimidated by such a list, but over the years we have also found that one of the great distinguishing characteristics of environment and natural resource professionals and leaders is their passion for and commitment to their work. It is this sense of wanting to make a difference, wanting to manage natural resources in ways that ensure their long sustainability, that motivates those who choose this profession and who are willing and able to develop the skills and characteristics for successful leadership.

Another set of survey questions asked respondents to agree or disagree with twelve specific statements about leadership (Table 2.1). For example, 94 percent of the respondents agreed that different people will lead at different times in the same organization, regardless of organizational hierarchy or structure. This means, at the least, that our leaders saw leadership as a function diffused throughout an organization, and not the sole property of leaders designated by position or title. We think this is particularly important because it means that each member of an organization must be practically prepared to lead when his or her turn or time comes.

Interestingly, gender differences were seen to be important to our leadership group. Men and women have predictably different leadership skills and styles, according to 84 percent of our respondents. Furthermore, in spite of the shift in the 1990s to a more participatory and shared decision-making model for natural resource policy, 71 percent agreed that "command-and-control leadership is still necessary at times."

We find this continuing need for, at times, a more authoritarian leadership approach reflects some of our change in perspective as well. Increased public participation and involvement is a matter of fact and practice for today's environmental leaders. However, participatory leadership requires time and resources, and given the contentious nature of environmental issues, sometimes can generate more process than timely result. Perhaps as a consequence, survey respondents believed that leaders today are more process ori-

TABLE 2.1. **Environmental leaders' responses to selected survey questions.**

	Strongly Agree 5	(5+4)	Agree 4	Neither Agree/ Disagree 3	Disagree 2	(2+1)	Strongly Disagree 1
In most organizations, leadership needs to be attributed to one identifiable person.	2	(37%)	9	4 (13%)	11	(50%)	4
Men and women often have different leadership skills and styles.	5	(84%)	21	1 (3%)	4	(13%)	0
The problem with today's leadership is that no one is accountable.	1	(20%)	5	12 (40%)	11	(40%)	1
Within an organization, different people will lead at different times.	12	(94%)	17	1 (3%)	1	(3%)	0
Important leadership skills usually stay constant regardless of situation.	3	(39%)	9	3 (10%)	14	(51%)	2
In general, we have less evident environmental leadership today than in the past.	3	(45%)	11	1 (3%)	15	(52%)	1
Leaders today are more process, rather than product, oriented.	3	(58%)	15	10 (32%)	1	(10%)	2

Statement	1		2	3	4		5
Environmental leadership is basically no different than other kinds of leadership (e.g., leadership in business or the military).	2	(35%)	9	4 (13%)	13	(52%)	3
"Command-and-control" leadership is still necessary at times.	6	(71%)	16	6 (19%)	2	(10%)	1
Leaders cannot lead without authority.	4	(35%)	7	3 (10%)	14	(55%)	3
Some leadership skills can be taught, but most are innate and intuitive.	3	(58%)	15	3 (10%)	9	(32%)	1
Leadership today is more difficult than in the past.	9	(71%)	13	1 (3%)	5	(26%)	3

Note: Leaders rated on a scale of 1 to 5 (1 = strongly disagree, 5 = strongly agree), how much they agreed or disagreed with each statement. Numbers without parentheses are number of respondents; numbers with parentheses are percent total responses.

Survey respondents cited several sorts of environmental problems in which they thought classic command-and-control leadership probably worked well and was necessary. Two of these were problem-solving activities often described as done by "paramilitary" organizations: wildfire fighting and law enforcement. The third area was development activities in some developing countries. A "command-and-control" leadership style tends to be associated with situations in which uncertainty is high and consequences of "wrong" decisions and actions may be dire or lethal. Thus, increased certainty is traded against greater flexibility and creativity. It is interesting to note, however, that military organizations, regarded as applying the distilled essence of command-and-control leadership, value individual leadership highly and strive to instill the ability to "take the initiative" in fluid and uncertain situations.

Source: Leader Survey quote.

ented than in the past. However, the majority also said that "good environmental leadership is evident and that leaders are able to lead without authority."

Perhaps one of the most provocative survey results is that 58 percent agreed that "some leadership skills can be taught but most are innate and intuitive." We find this a particularly good area for further exploration given our strong conviction that leadership skills and styles can be learned. Also, respondents' opinions were fairly well split about the statement "Environmental leadership is basically no different than other kinds of leadership."

Another crucial area related to identification of leadership skills and styles is an understanding of how leaders emerge in environmental and natural resources organizations. Our leaders described a broad spectrum of organizational approaches (or non-approaches) to the recognition and cultivation of potential leaders. One end of the spectrum is a formal and focused approach to leadership development. For instance:

> We recruit individuals with a record of academic accomplishment and leadership in high school and college. In our interview process, we look for interest in advancing as a manager and not just a technical focus. Second, during the first couple of years on the job, we observe and counsel individuals with an emphasis on team activity and a willingness to "take charge" and "take ownership of projects and activities." Third, we place emphasis on job rotation and continuing education to

develop those who emerge from the first two steps. In other words, we create a climate for leadership to emerge.

These organizations with more focused approaches rely on job-based performance and advancement through increasing levels of responsibility to form leaders. "Leaders emerge who consistently meet the expectations of the organization. They help define problems, design solutions, and achieve positive results with ever increasing complexity." In turn, organizations offer formalized leadership development and mentoring programs.

The other end of the spectrum was described as "leaders by accident" or "survival of the fittest." In these organizations, leaders get very little training or few career development opportunities. They often emerge by "self-definition" or "personality." Entrepreneurship and risk taking appear to be key in organizations in which those seeking leadership opportunities need to "promote their own self interests" *or* "emerge out of the situational mix of the moment."

Our respondents identified several other opportunities for leadership to emerge:

- "A combination of character and opportunity. Leaders 'ripen' but they need a disposition tilted toward passion and action."

- "Through service and display of leadership qualities in significant committee work."

- "Ability to separate emotion from action."

- "Through networking and doing a good (superior) job where they are today. Too many people plot their whole career and fail to accomplish everyday goals."

- "High ability to seek solutions inside and outside the organization."

- "Having clear intellectual ideas of needed directions for resource management and policy that are in harmony with real societal needs."

The message from our leaders was that there is no one recipe for how leaders emerge in the diverse array of environment and natural resource organizations. The key for potential leaders is an understanding of the leadership culture of an organization and how they can best display their leadership achievements and potential in that environment.

Overall, our leader survey revealed agreement about a world much changed in a bit less than a decade, and thought leadership has become more difficult as a result. Respondents also reaffirmed a core set of leadership characteristics and skills, and a wide diversity of organizational attitudes toward the development of new leadership, which they saw (not surprisingly) as the most critical task facing current leaders. They strongly felt that publics were more contentious and less well educated about environment and natural resource issues. In sum, environmental leadership challenges abound.

Essentials

 The context for today's leadership is shaped by globalization, population, and demographic changes; shifts in public values and ethics; the role of government, economic, and social policy; the technological revolution, environmental complexity, and education.

 Communication, listening, and interpersonal skills are the most important leadership characteristics.

 Today's leaders must be educated about the human dimensions of environmental problems as well as the biological and technological.

 Different people will lead at different times regardless of organizational hierarchy or structure.

 Gender differences continue to significantly influence leadership skills and styles.

 There is not a single or consistent model of how leaders are cultivated or emerge in organizations.

Chapter 3

Essential Leadership Attributes

 The most important personal leadership characteristics to nurture and practice are:

- Vision, the ability to see ahead and communicate what you see
- Information, the ability to find, understand, and transmit needed information
- Inclusion, listening and using all available skills and ideas
- Decision, defining and pursuing an action agenda
- Dispatch, doing things now rather than later
- Standard setting, formulating the definition of success
- Humanity, using empathy and humor in dealing with others

We think that creating a shared vision is the key to environmental leadership. This can involve the construction of formal vision or mission statements. The core activity, however, is the definition of the problem or problems to be solved and the construction of the group and strategy to solve it for them. It really involves creating a dynamic view of what the best solution will look like, and when it will be ready. It is also important to know what the solution will cost in both financial and human terms. Trying to see through to the consequences of solving the problem is difficult but necessary. What happens if the problem isn't solved? If it is, who wins and who loses? What is the likelihood of effects on other people and organizations removed from the immediate problem? We advocate creating and filling in a "vision table" in which each of these questions is answered. The table then becomes the dynamic picture of the state of problem knowledge and solution.

The greater availability of information is one of the factors that makes environmental leadership methods imperative, and it is also a leadership problem. The huge flow of information from science and practical experience is now

TABLE 3.1. **A sample vision table.**

Problem element	Approach 1	Approach 2	Approach 3	Approach rank
Outcomes Direct benefits Direct costs Risk factors Time to solution				
Team requirements Disciplines Number of people Communication Location				
Total cost People Operations Travel Capital goods Overhead Consequences Winners Losers Side effects				

A vision table describes how a visualized goal can be approached, and compares the approaches in terms of outcomes, team requirements, cost, and consequences. A leader will create the table, use it to communicate with her team, and update it periodically. Creation of a vision table will also help discriminate against purely wishful visions, by indicating the difficulty of realizing them. A vision table is an intermediate step between a "notion" and a fully worked-out project plan, and thus is an informal, but fairly rigorous, tool.

readily available in theory through the Internet, libraries, journals, books, and courses. Unless there is a system and people to screen and channel the flow to the elements of the problem, the flow can become a flood that washes away any purpose other than keeping up with it. One cliché has it that keeping up with current information is like "drinking from a fire hose." But just as no one in their right mind would attempt to quench their thirst that way, no one should approach information as an end in itself. The leader knows what needs to be known to solve the problem and screens out or diverts the rest. It is often useful to construct an "information needs diagram" during problem definition. This identifies, for each of the five "solvable problem" elements described in Chapter 4, information needs and likely generic sources.

Groups or teams work well only when each member's full potential is exposed and used. Ideally, the group formed to solve a problem is chosen based on the problem's characteristics. Once the group is chosen, it is important to redefine the problem using the full resources of the group. During this process the leader becomes adept at listening to

TABLE 3.2. **An information table.**

Problem element	Needed information			Source
Decision maker	Characteristics	Numbers	Locations	DM direct contact
Objective	Statement	Time available	Money available	DM direct contact
Alternatives	Time and cost	Feasibility	Risk	DM plus other sources
Doubt	Cause	Depth	Level of uncertainty	Who doubts
Context	Organization	Location	Social environment	Observation

Each problem element requires the collection of information. The best and most useful source is the decision maker who has the problem, but direct communication is not always possible. If not, secondary sources—documents, helpers, commentators, and critics—need to be consulted.

all members of this specific group, and extracting from them all their ideas and knowledge that bear on the problem (this process is sometimes known as "group consulting"). Once chosen in light of the problem, the more diverse a group is, the more likely it is to have within it quality solutions because it will have a wider range of experience and expertise.

Of course, other things are never equal, and usually the more diverse a group is the harder it is to manage.

A good leader will balance diversity and manageability. We have used an informal matrix for achieving this balance based on fundamental characteristics of those in the group. The matrix classifies people as completers or noncompleters in the columns and whether they make the group's life easier or harder in the rows. "Completers" are people who almost always finish what they start or tasks they are given in the time allotted. "Noncompleters" may be brilliant people who make valuable contributions, but who almost never do anything on time or within budget. "Life easier" people tend to be optimistic, companionable, and easy to work with. They may or may not top the list in substance. "Life harder" people, who again may be highly effective and valuable in other ways, tend to see the dark side of things, raise all possible objections to a course of action, and have prickly personalities. In this oversimplified, somewhat tongue-in-cheek, but amazingly useful, method, the leader's first task is to move the "noncompleter/life harder" people out of the group. The second task is to ensure the "completer/life easier" set is adequately rewarded and supported. The third task is strike a balance between the "life easier/noncompleter" and the "life harder/completer" groups so that neither dominates, and to manage their interaction carefully.

Defining and implementing an action agenda in the context of a group solving a specific problem is a continuing task for the group's leader or leaders. Once an important decision is made, it is a good idea to construct a detailed implementation plan. One useful form for this is to list the implementation tasks in order of their start dates, estimate completion dates for each, and present them in a calendar format. Doing things now (that is, on time) rather than later

TABLE 3.3. **A group composition matrix.**

	Life easier	*Life harder*
Completer	Reward, keep	Balance
Noncompleter	Balance	Remove

The success of groups in solving environmental problems is determined more by their composition than any other factor. An environmental leader takes full advantage of his or her ability to shape a group into an effective entity. This matrix calls for the classification of each actual or potential group member into one of the four categories above, and leadership action to see that those in the lower right box are removed, those in the upper left box are rewarded, and those in the other two boxes balance each other. This will not solve all group problems, but it will make the leader and the group members better able to concentrate on and complete the tasks at hand.

(that is, after they should have been done) is sometimes seen as mundane and unfashionable. But procrastination is one of the most common causes of leadership failure. The simple injunction is, having decided on an action, take it. One of the ways to track this is to take the planned action agenda as diagrammed below and overlay on it when tasks are actually initiated and completed.

Those who set standards for organizational performance, the use of technical tools, environmental improvement, and success in problem solving create for themselves and their organization a leadership position. By definition, those who comply with standards set by others are following, not leading. But more important, commitment to being a standard setter constantly challenges a group to be better than their competition or, indeed, themselves. Also, constantly changing standards demand constant attention, which keeps leaders and organizations focused on change and generally on their toes.

The need to produce integrated solutions using deliberately diverse groups maximally challenges the human relation skills of the leader. People from different disciplines

TABLE 3.4. **A simple action agenda.**

Task (in order of start date)	Time (days, months, or years as appropriate)
	1 2 3 4 5 6 7 8 9 10 11 12 13 14 15 16 17 18 19 20
Task 1	--------C---------------------
Task 2	--------------------------------C
Task 3	----------------------C------
Task ..n	------------C

This format allows the tracking of both intended and actual completion times for separate group tasks. The intended start and completion times are indicated by the beginning and end of the dashed lines, and actual completion dates by a letter C.

and experience groups tend to speak different languages and to value different ideas and modes of thought and behavior. The first "human relations" task of the good leader is to review his or her own conduct and language for signals that will be considered unnecessarily adverse or exclusionary by others. We say "unnecessarily" because the substance of ideas and techniques must not be corrupted or "watered down" in the name of better group dynamics. Indeed, it is imperative for the leader to make his or her substantive views and techniques important to problem solution clear to the group.

When, inevitably, there are differences in the group on how to proceed because of different disciplinary or experiential knowledge, these differences must be discussed and resolved. The use of humor can be important to illustrate and resolve differences, if used naturally and without malice. Self-deprecating humor from the leader can be an effective way to get others to talk freely. But our advice is to leave telling set piece jokes to professional comedians. Most jokes disparage somebody or some idea. If you are not Seinfeld, don't go there. It is productive, usually, to try sincerely to see why people could hold a point of view that seems wrong or out of place to you.

Personal leadership traits are necessarily embedded in each personality, but they can be changed in positive ways by study and practice. Just keeping the list of leadership traits at the beginning of the chapter in mind can help in this. Improvement in this way is particularly aided by talking with friends candidly. "After-action analyses" are particularly valuable. In these, you seek feedback about how you performed in a given situation, and relate your performance to the leadership characteristics. No one known to us possesses all the characteristics in optimum amounts; the only practical approach is one of continuous review and improvement.

Essentials

 Essential leadership characteristics are vision, information, inclusion, decision, dispatch, standard setting, and humanity.

 Creating a shared vision is the key to environmental leadership.

 Problem definition followed by the construction of a group and strategy to solve the problem are core leadership activities.

 Creating a vision table, information needs diagram, group matrix, action agenda, and implementation plan will guide integrated problem solving.

 Commit to being a standard setter.

 Study and practice will produce positive essential leadership attributes.

Chapter 4

Solving Environmental Problems: Long Times and Complexity

Environmental leaders are those who solve environmental problems using the resources of organizations, so problem definition is central to environmental leadership. In Chapters 4 and 5 we describe how environmental problems are defined and how, in turn, definitions shape solutions.

Most environmental problems are first described as belonging to large classes that include general threats to the environment, such as "air pollution," "water quality," or "deforestation." To be solvable, however, each instance within a class must have its own complete definition. We rely heavily on examples from our own experience to illustrate this. All of these involve forests and the controversies and opportunities that surround them. Obviously, that is partly because much of our experience is with forests and the people who care about them. But we think there is another reason, equally valid, for our use of forest examples. Forests are complex systems that profoundly affect all components of the human environment: air and water quality, open space, industrial raw material, and the human spirit, to name a few. As one international leader put it, "When you touch the forest, you touch everything."

We think all solvable problems, environmental or not, have five elements that must be specified carefully and completely (Ackoff 1962):

- A decision maker
- An objective that the decision maker wishes to achieve
- A range of alternative ways to achieve the objective
- Doubt about which alternative to choose
- A context in which the first four above are contained

Once a problem is defined in terms of these elements, it is solved when the decision maker makes the correct (ef-

fective) choice among alternatives and successfully imple-
ments that decision.

The decision maker can be a single individual, or class
of individuals, or it can be an organization, such as a firm
or a government agency. To meet the criteria of problem
definition, however, it must be "real." That is, the decision
maker must have a known location, and be able to take in
and respond to information. The objective must be concrete,
meaning that it is stated so that it is possible to know when
it is achieved. It can be quantitative or qualitative, near term
or long term, expensive or inexpensive, but the amount of
time and money estimated to be needed for its achievement
must be stated as accurately as possible. The alternative paths
to the achievement of the objective must also be "real" in
the sense that they are plausible and achievable. For some
problems, no alternative meets these criteria, and then the
core of the problem becomes finding acceptable alternatives.
This often involves primary scientific research, and this is
one good reason why environmental (and other) leaders
need to be familiar with and connected to sources of primary
research. Doubt about which alternative to choose is often

> The first requirement of decision making is that you do it. There is never enough information or enough time, but nothing undermines the reputation of a leader faster than the perception that you avoid hard decisions. . . . Good decision making is especially important in a field where many issues are both technically complex and politically sensitive. . . . Decision makers get into trouble when they disregard the legal or policy framework for the decision, when they ignore (or seem to ignore) pertinent facts and opinions, or when they give no reasons (or phony reasons) for their choices. Even people who are adversely affected can often accept a decision they think is wrong. What rankles is an impression that they have not been heard or that a hidden agenda has dictated the outcome."

Source: L. Carothers. 1993. "Leadership in State Agencies." In J. Berry and J. Gordon, eds. *Environmental Leadership: Developing Effective Skills and Styles,* 157. Washington, D.C., and Covelo, Calif.: Island Press.

quantified as the risk of choosing wrongly or the risk of inaction. If there are no adverse consequences of a wrong choice, or of choosing no action (ignoring the "problem") then, in our definition, there is no problem. Allocating resources to solving non-problems is poor leadership. To de-

> **D**evelop and strengthen your knowledge of links between resources/environmental matters and successful functions of national and regional economies. With such understanding you will be fairly rare and valuable."
>
> *Source:* Leader Survey quote.

scribe the context of the problem, those elements of the decision maker's environment that bear on the problem must be described. These can include anything from physical location and conditions to laws, regulations, and policies. Failure to understand how actions to solve a problem interact with important elements of its environment is the shortest route to adverse unintended consequences.

In *Environmental Leadership: Developing Effective Skills and Styles,* we concluded that environmental problems commonly have five additional characteristics, and we have since added another. These six are:

- Long time from perception of the problem to its useful definition and solution;
- Complexity in most dimensions, including knowledge

required, kinds of people involved, and multiplicity of the effects of any solution;

- A contentious and emotion-charged context, with definite and different values held by participants;

- A need for integration across several to many areas of knowledge;

- An often weak and scattered science base that presents few "school solutions" for problems; and

- Surprises and unintended consequences on the way to solution.

An environmental problem is fully defined, then, in our terms, when the five "solvable problem" and six "environmental problem" criteria have been specified correctly. For the "environmental problem" the criteria can derived from the characteristics with these questions:

- What is the estimated time to solution, and what are the major activities to which the estimated time will be allocated?

- What are the major complex elements and systems involved in the problem and its solution, how do they work, and how are they controlled?

- What are the human elements (factions, values, organizations) that will aid or impede solving the problem?

- What are the major disciplinary areas of knowledge that will need to be integrated to specify solutions?

- What is the specific science base available to the problem solvers, and how can it best be accessed?

- Surprises and unintended consequences cannot by their nature be predicted, but what surprises and unintended consequences can now be imagined, and how would they be handled?

Several of the assessments in which we have participated illustrate all the six characteristics well. Each case, although it exhibits all six, is chosen because we feel it illustrates one of them particularly well.

The Pacific Northwest controversy about old-growth forests on federal lands illustrates the "long time from per-

---

The world is so much more complex than it used to be, and the amounts of information we have to sift through are so vast. It also runs faster and economic shifts impact people, their work, and their lives very quickly. No one person can 'run' anything of any significant size any more and 'be the boss.' We have to work as teams, appreciate the expertise each person brings to the team, and be prepared to stand back and let different people with different kinds of skills step forward to contribute their part when called for."

Source: Leader Survey quote.

ception to definition and solution" especially well. Most of the magnificent old conifer forests of the Pacific Slope that still existed in the late twentieth century were on federal land. Environmental groups were calling for their preservation from harvest. The federal land management agencies, principally the USDA Forest Service and the Bureau of Land Management, were undergoing intensive planning for the future of these forests, and were striving to preserve their commitment to "multiple use," which called for the harvest of at least some of the old forests. The agencies were supported in this by industry and community interests committed to retaining a vigorous wood products industry and the jobs and economic benefits it could provide. The Northwest Forest Plan was a solution to the old-growth controversy in the sense that it resulted in the lifting of court-imposed sanctions on federal forestry (FEMAT 1993, Tuchman et al. 1996). But it evolved in stages from a scientific beginning in research accelerated or initiated in the Coniferous Forest Biome program in the 1970s, and progressed through a series of organizationally and congressionally sponsored assessments to its proclamation by the Clinton administration in 1993. The old-growth controversy also illustrates that different decision makers see different problems and have different objectives when viewing the same situation. For example, federal agencies wanted the court injunctions lifted so their "normal" program activities, particularly timber harvest, could proceed. Environmental groups wanted more old growth on federal lands protected from harvest. Industry groups wanted to ensure timber supply from federal lands, and to prevent federal forest management styles and rules from being applied to private land. Here, we briefly follow the federal agency path, because they were charged with making decisions about the forests in question by the federal Congress, and had been blocked from doing so by the federal courts. Thus the "solvable criteria" could be stated as:

- The decision maker was the leadership of the lead federal agency, the USDA Forest Service.
- The objective was to have a land allocation and management strategy on federal land that would result in the federal courts viewing their actions as legal and appropriate under federal laws (the National Forest Management Act and the Endangered Species Act, principally, but many others as well).

- Alternatives to achieve their objective could be stated in the form of alternative rules for forest management, particularly the relationship between timber harvest and wildlife habitat protection, since old-growth habitat for two birds, the northern spotted owl and the marbled murrelet, had become the central contended issue.

- Doubt about which alternative rules to adopt turned practically on what the courts would accept, and at the inception of the problem there was no ready way to describe this. Thus the provision of new alternatives became urgent.

- The context included all the federal forests of the "west side" of the Cascade Mountains and Coast Range in Oregon, Washington, and Northern California. It also included all the environmental and industry groups and all the federal agencies concerned, as well as the many laws, policies, and regulations in force for those lands at that time.

The environmental criteria were easily specified and made the problem doubly difficult. Although the science that exposed the biology of old-growth forests in the Pacific Northwest and its hitherto unknown importance as owl and murrelet habitat was begun in the late 1960s, the scientific picture was unclear into the 1990s. Most scientists admitted that the science on which to base new rules for harvest and land allocation was still weak. Wildlife biologists and silviculturists and other timber management experts didn't communicate well among themselves and had done few integrated studies of timber harvest and its effects on wildlife. In addition to the two birds, salmon habitat and the effects of timber harvest on spawning and rearing streams were emerging issues. However, the new federal administration wanted the problem solved as rapidly as possible. The atmosphere was tense. Contending interest groups traded threats and law suits. Clearly the science base was weaker than was desirable. Knowledge about timber harvest and habitat needed to be integrated, the time to problem solution was being arbitrarily shortened by administration fiat, and both the natural and policy systems involved were acknowledged by all to be almost hopelessly complex. But the federal objective was achieved, and in that sense, the problem was solved, roughly in the time allowed.

A series of assessments of the situation or parts of it began to integrate the available information and create new alternatives for rules and allocations through synthesis and interdisciplinary cooperation. These culminated in 1993 in the Northwest Forest Plan, which was promulgated by the administration through an interagency task force. These new rules were accepted by the federal courts as responsive to their prior rulings, and the agencies, principally the USDA Forest Service and the Bureau of Land Management, were free to manage the federal lands under the new rules. It is fair to say that none of the participants were wholly satisfied with the solution. Predictably, the environmental groups did not feel that enough federal forest had been additionally protected. Just as predictably, timber industry groups, loggers, and local communities that depended economically on timber harvest thought the new rules didn't provide for nearly enough timber harvest. Many federal managers felt the rules were difficult or impossible to carry out effectively. But the problem as originally stated, the lifting of the federal injunction against timber harvest, was solved, at least for a time.

We, the authors, were directly and indirectly involved in the process for most of its existence, and still are. As we write, the agencies involved are doing the ten-year evaluation of the Northwest Forest Plan. Opinion is predictably split on the overall "goodness" of the plan and its effects, but an overwhelming majority would agree that it has had a major impact on the region in which it was implemented in terms of both timber supply and habitat. We think much was, and still is being, learned. What were the leadership actions that contributed most directly to the solution? The assessments that lead up to the formal plan are one of the keys. These took existing knowledge and put it in a framework that could be used by policy makers. One, the Scientific Panel on Late Successional Forests (Johnson et al. 1991), was created by an extraordinarily bold action of a congressional committee. They reached out directly to the scientific community to create a panel of scientists to describe the whole problem, including not just timber harvest and the birds, but salmon as well, and to provide a range of alternative solutions with predicted outcomes and risk levels. Although Congress found itself unable to act on the recommendations of the panel, the administration picked up its findings almost whole and incorporated them into the Northwest Forest Plan.

Thus, the key leadership actions were the congressional decision to create the panel and the administration's decision to use its results, along with those of a series of assessments of the key species involved. Both decisions required a sophisticated knowledge of both politics and science and involved considerable risk. Although the "solvability" and "environmental" problem definition elements were not formally identified, all were treated implicitly, and a solution, however imperfect (remember, no final solutions occur) resulted.

The current concern about urban sprawl and the "wildland-urban interface" (WUI) recently has been brought to broad public attention by huge wildfires, mainly in the West, that also destroy hundreds of private homes. This "interface" is primarily the tension between the management of urban expansion ("sprawl") and large areas of forest. The urban and forest systems are each dauntingly complex, and together they well illustrate the compound complexity of environmental problems. Again, different stakeholders define the problem differently, and it is fair to say that there is no overall agreement even on the general nature of the problem. The multiplicity of decision makers and decision maker objectives makes this an especially interesting problem.

Decision makers with a stake in solving this problem include public and private wildland owners and managers, developers, homeowners, federal, state and urban govern-ments, insurers, environmental advocacy groups, and many others.

Their objectives are many, but a common objective is to minimize loss due to the interaction of urban expansion and the management regimes practiced on wildland. The in-teraction between this often shared goal and the individual goals of decision makers determines outcomes. For example, a developer wants to subdivide and build houses on rural land to provide housing for people and to make a profit. He can incur loss when unsold homes or lots burn, or when zoning rules reduce options for development. Environmental groups may oppose timber harvest on WUI forests in the interest of habitat or ecology, but risk losing support and credibility if people whose houses burn up blame their ad-vocacy for the fire.

Alternatives for achieving the common objective range from the absolutes of preventing all urban expansion into wildlands through zoning or voluntary prohibitions, to the fireproofing (insofar as possible) of forests through forest and fire management. To be seriously considered from a political point of view, real solutions will lie between these and in their combination.

Doubt exists in general about what combinations of urban restrictions and forest management will work politically and in technical, on-the-ground terms. Overlaid on this general uncertainty is the vast array of different local conditions and rules that prevail at the many WUIs.

The context adds its own complexity, in that the general problem is seen differently in different urban settings and ecosystems. Fire is the predominant concern in the inland West. In the Northeast, loss of open space and possible adverse economic consequences of development for local taxpayers are the main concerns. Local zoning laws, public land management strategies, the mix of public and private land, among other things, vary with locality.

Probably no event in environmental management is more emotionally charged than a large forest fire. By the time a fire is large enough to make the evening news, there is little hope of putting it out by purely human efforts, and even containment may be elusive for days or weeks depending on the weather and forest conditions. The perception and often the reality is an event that threatens life and property that is out of human control. On the other hand, the urbanization of wildland has been likened to a glacier: an inexorable, but often slow, advance. The contrast between the rapid devastation caused by fire and the usually slow (time scale of years) advance of the urban front illustrates well the complexity of environmental problem solving. Environmental leadership is clearly needed to fashion local solutions but also to find a vector or framework for approaching the general problem. The Healthy Forests initiative promulgated by the Bush (43) administration is an attempt at such leadership and is being debated and implemented as we write.

These are U.S.-based examples, but similar ones could be drawn from many countries and all continents except Antarctica. The evolution of the European problem of the effects of acid rain from the then-Soviet bloc countries of central and eastern Europe on the forests of western Europe has a similar time scale and complexity, for example.

These two vignettes of environmental problems are simplified but, we think, accurate within that limit. They clearly illustrate the long gestation time of major environmental problems and their grinding complexity. Environmental leaders must first be aware of these, and then use the analytical tools above to render them tractable, or at least understandable. Environmental leaders use these methods to make the right decision and to support its implementation, often over very long times and against very high odds.

Essentials

 An environmental problem is defined when the five solvable problem criteria and the six environmental problem criteria are correctly specified and understood.

 Perception is everything. Different decision makers see different problems and have different objectives when viewing the same situation.

 Integration of science is key. Scientists from different disciplines—natural, physical, and social—need to continually integrate their work and communicate with each other often and well.

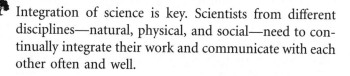 Time frames for science, management, and policy are not equal. Decision makers and managers require the results of science more quickly than the science process often allows. In general, major environmental problems are defined by long gestation times and grinding com-

plexity, and all involved need to understand the boundary conditions of their specific problem and process.

🌳 Synthesis of science can provide important information for decision makers. Science assessments are an effective way to review the current state of science and to provide timely options for decision making (see previous Essential).

🌳 Total human satisfaction is not a common attribute of environmental problem solutions. Most solutions arise from compromise among deeply held values and objectives, and most likely no one group will believe that all their needs and objectives have been met. But all participants should feel these solutions are better in some way.

Chapter 5

Solving Environmental Problems: Emotion, Values, Integration, and Focus

In this chapter we examine two more examples from our experience in terms of our problem definition elements and try to derive leadership lessons from them. As in Chapter 4, both are complex sets of human activities related to complicated ecosystems and ideas. We have tried to summarize them accurately; the sources we cite at the end of the book can provide a much fuller (but still not complete) understanding of them.

The Seventh American Forest Congress (SAFC) (Bentley and Langbein 1996) was an attempt to bring together all the stakeholders in American forests who were willing to concentrate on finding things to agree on concerning the future of America's forests, if there were any things to agree upon, rather than arguing. Consensus was not the goal, but rather to see whether people across the spectrum of views about forests (environmentalists, industry people, resource professionals, concerned citizens) could find any common ground. This effort, which took over two years, from 1994 through the first half of 1996, illustrated graphically the strongly held values and emotion-charged context in which environmental leaders work. But it also showed that people with vastly different values and experience can agree when allowed the time and surroundings to listen to each other.

The SAFC posed two key questions about America's for-

Barriers to environmental leadership include the "increase of systems of belief that have no room for compromise or differences of opinion," and the "proliferation of ego-centered self-interests that impede the forming of common-good consensus in issue after issue and lack of civility in nearly all collective processes."

Source: Leader Survey quote.

ests: "What is our common vision?" and "What principles do we agree upon to guide us toward our vision?" The goal was to assess what common ground there might be for a national forest policy. The process was inclusive. Roundtables (at least one in all states but two, with New England acting as a unit) preceded a three-and-a-half day gathering of about 1,500 people in Washington, D.C. Registration was open to all, and financial assistance was provided for those who needed it. A wide spectrum of those who saw themselves as "forest stakeholders" attended. National and local environmental groups, private landowners, tribal people, forest products industry people, and resource professionals were all included in the state and national meetings. This in itself was significant because attendance was completely voluntary. The roundtable process assigned seats at tables of eight to ten people on the basis of a "max mix" principle. Each table represented a mixture of geography, interests, experience, and values. Individual agendas varied with the descriptors of diversity with all participants cautioned that they were representing themselves. Rough degree of agreement on vision elements and principles at both the table and congress level was expressed as colors: green, full agreement; yellow, mixed feelings but acceptable; red, disagreement, don't accept.

The results demonstrated major agreement on most elements of a common vision, and on a large number of principles to support the vision. During the Congress many of the vision elements and principles were redrafted, and levels of agreement thus increased.

SAFC was launched and carried out by a self-appointed group of leaders from academia, environmental NGOs, government agencies, and the forest products industry. Feelings ran high throughout the process and at the Washington meeting, but ultimate levels of agreement were far higher than anyone expected or predicted at the outset. But the goal of redrafting American forest policy was not met, or at least hasn't been at the time of this writing.

The decision makers who were intended to be served by SAFC were ultimately the United States Congress, the sovereign body responsible for national forest policy. Because such a policy would have to be bipartisan to succeed (or so the reasoning went), members of Congress and their helpers, and, indeed, political appointees of the then-current administration, were excluded. Thus, the organizers felt that neither party could claim ownership or exclusion.

The objective that the SAFC sought at the outset was to have Congress reconsider and revise the mostly old and uncoordinated (because they were passed at different times for different purposes) laws that governed United States forest policy. These included the National Forest Management Act (1976), the Multiple Use and Sustained Yield Act (1960), the Endangered Species Act (1973), and the National Environmental Policy Act (1969), among others. It was thought that the only way such a comprehensive and integrated effort could be sustained would be through demonstrating to Congress that a broad coalition of people interested in forests, particularly including environmental organizations and the forest products industry, shared a strong common vision for America's forests.

Several alternative ways to create this vision were considered, but it was finally decided that only the most inclusive process affordable (SAFC was privately funded by companies, foundations, academic institutions, and individuals) would credibly meet the objective. Thus the state roundtable process and the Washington meeting were designed with inclusiveness and diversity as major principles. A strict time schedule was imposed, primarily to provide results that made sense in terms of the national legislative calendar.

There was clear doubt at the outset whether a common vision and set of principles could be found. Many felt that the differences in values and experience across the spectrum of people interested in forests was too great to expect any agreement. Almost all debate among forest stakeholders had been focused on points of contention, many of them related to timber harvest on federal forests. Little progress had been observed in this for a decade. However, SAFC organizers were convinced that looking for areas of agreement between factions had never really been tried. There was also a view, later supported, that groups important to the future of forests were not previously engaged in the debate.

The context in which SAFC took place included the acrimonious, long-standing debate over public forests, a set of laws directly and indirectly regulating forests that arose over many years with little coordination, and all the geographic scope and ecological complexity of all the forests in America.

SAFC was a deliberate attempt by an initially small, self-selected group to exercise environmental leadership. It ultimately involved thousands of individuals from many backgrounds. It did produce a reasonably well-agreed vision and set of principles upon which national forest policy could have been (and still could be) constructed. It produced a new awareness that most of America's forests were privately owned, and that most of those were owned by so-called non-industrial owners (those who didn't own wood processing facilities). Also, it showed that urban people, those with the most political influence, had not been engaged in the debate over forest policy to a very great degree. What it did not do, or at least hasn't yet, is precipitate a comprehensive review and rewriting of American forest policy. Perhaps the most important leadership lesson to be learned from it is to include in the problem definition and attempts at solution the designated decision makers (in this case, members of Congress and their helpers). The SAFC organizers chose to exclude legislators from the process, and undoubtedly partly as a result of this, its results were for the most part ignored by them. Although several presentations of SAFC outcomes were made to members of the Senate and House, and a number of legislators listened politely and even with interest, no one picked up the vision and led a legislative initiative.

To illustrate the need for integration across areas of knowledge, and the handicap that a weak and scattered science base is, we have chosen an assessment of vegetation management goals for elk winter range in Rocky Mountain National Park. Both the structure and the outcome of this assessment taught us much. In this park, elk numbers had reached controversial levels. Not only were they heavily browsing (to an ecologically damaging level, in the eyes of some) park vegetation, primarily aspen and willow, they were also heavily impacting a thickly settled area south of the part (Estes Park, Colorado). Elk visited golf courses, parking lots, backyards, and city streets, causing both a tourist attraction and deep angst. As one resident said, "Anything larger than me that isn't frightened of me frightens me." Clearly, elk numbers were, in the eyes of some, a problem both inside and outside the park. To others, they were a marvelous manifestation of the fecundity and beauty of nature and superb "watchable wildlife" to boot.

Several steps were taken to carefully define the problem and to pose alternative solutions. First, scientists from a wide array of disciplines brought together what is known about elk, their habitat, and their interactions in the vicinity of Rocky Mountain National Park. When this synthesis was complete, a small panel worked with park managers to more closely define the problem and to offer alternative solutions. The integration brought together a badly scattered science base that allowed a much stricter definition of the problem. From this base, the panel was able to construct plausible solutions that were consistent with Park Service policy.

The decision makers were the Park Service managers who are responsible for management of the park, particularly its vegetation and animals. They were the source of the request for the assessment, and participated throughout.

Their objective was to construct vegetation management goals in elk winter range for the park that would guide conservation of its existing vegetation types, particularly aspen and streamside willow, while at the same time main-

> **M**anaging across ecosystems requires a level of information and analysis that is generally lacking. Information needs to span political/agency/public/private boundaries and be available to everyone."
>
> *Source:* Leader Survey quote.

taining an elk herd of a size appropriate to the vegetation management goals. A parallel objective was to determine the impact of elk numbers outside the park, and particularly on the heavily settled area around Estes Park.

Alternatives for achieving the objectives included primarily "natural regulation" in which the elk herd and the vegetation would come into some natural balance without management activities, "vegetation management" in which efforts would be made to reduce elk impact on specific communities by making them less palatable, or increasing their size, and "elk management" in which elk numbers would be reduced by culling the herd. Although elements of each would probably make up some component of any practical alternative, many proponents of "natural regulation" and "elk management" considered these alternatives to be mutually exclusive.

Doubt about what alternative to devise in detail and implement had its source in two places. First, the opposition between those who favored "natural regulation" and "elk management" had heavy political implications. Many held the positions to be entirely outside any potential compromise. The "natural regulation" people argued that national parks are supposed to be examples of wild nature, so that "management," at least of the natural resources, was indelibly out of place. The "elk management" people argued that the creation of the park and its effect on its surroundings (given the lush elk food supply in urban settings) had simply allowed elk to multiply beyond their natural herd size, and thus had to be reduced. At the same time, there had been little attempt to bring together the science base of what was known about vegetation in the park and the elk herd.

The context was, as usual, emotionally charged. One possible outcome of an "elk management" alternative was to shoot enough elk to bring the herd down to the size that wouldn't threaten the park's vegetation. Shooting "protected" animals is always controversial. Similarly, park managers charged with maintaining the integrity of park resources were bound to try hard to keep the existing array of vegetation types. Although the problem was in many respects intensely local, it had national implications, since similar situations existed in other national parks.

The people who conducted the assessment, after listening to the leading scientists in the area present a synthesis of their findings, recommended the pursuit of several goals, including changing the impact of elk feeding on vegetation, restoring the role of fire in the park, gaining stakeholder support for active management, continuing ecosystem research on the Park as whole system, and better integrating research, monitoring, and management in the park. To pursue these goals, the panel recommended:

- An active management policy to reduce elk feeding in aspen, willow, shrub, and grassland communities;
- Public involvement in goal setting and management implementation and evaluation;
- Identifying and monitoring key indicators of vegetative conditions for an initial period of up to twenty years;

- More research on elk herbivory effects, especially at the landscape level;
- Suspending prescribed burns in these vegetation areas until herbivory is reduced and confidence is established that burns can occur without further degradation of vegetation types;
- A commitment to adaptive management (changing management as new information becomes available and using management activities to generate credible new information); and
- Effective educational communication that keeps the public informed about research and management activities in the park.

This assessment was conducted as the first step in a long-term adaptive management process and identified, for the first time, vegetation goals for the park. It resulted in the redirection of current research, including additional areas for research such as hydrology, and brought more emphasis to topic areas highlighted in the assessment. One of its major outcomes was providing the rationale for changing standard fire policy in these vegetation types until elk numbers are reduced. Overall, the assessment provided a framework for expanding willow and aspen protection and assessing elk grazing levels.

Perhaps the key leadership activity was the recognition of the "natural regulation" problem by park managers. They initiated a five-year research project focused on these concerns, and then convened the science synthesis and panel to make management recommendations three years into the research project. By doing this, they established closer communication among researchers, park managers, and publics. They also thus created a foundation for adaptive management activities that have since speeded learning about the problem. The Park Service initiators exhibited vision in their early recognition of and action on the problem. They were knowledgeable about where to seek information and help, and decisive in structuring the science synthesis and panel. And, they were ready to receive the results.

Essentials

🌳 Find agreement first, fight later. The first step in solving contentious environmental issues should be to seek areas of agreement, rather than focusing on issues that create an environment of polarization and friction.

🌳 A few courageous leaders with a commitment to problem solving can move beyond long-standing gridlock and conventional, but no longer effective, management practices.

🌳 Help the rational middle find its voice and power. Historically, bipolar points of view—often expressed as environmental versus economic or consumptive versus nonconsumptive—have exercised controlling influence over natural resource decisions. An inclusive, broad-based public involvement process will open the dialogue to those more willing to compromise and explore new solutions.

🌳 Bring everyone to the table. If policy or management change is the goal, decision makers and managers as well as a broad spectrum of stakeholders and citizens need to be active participants in the problem identification and solving process.

🌳 People with very different values and experiences can agree when given enough time and the opportunity to listen to each other. Establishing long-term partnerships among diverse organizations and people can overcome long-standing territorial and contentious habits and develop an environment of trust and shared decision making.

Chapter 6

From Old Leadership to
Essential Leadership

 From the base of experience provided by the survey and our own, we describe what we think is the essence of environmental leadership. A new or changed form of leadership arose and was first recognized in organizations with an environmental purpose because they were most often faced with problems that were long term, complex, and with a particular need for integration across disciplines. For example, the USDA Forest Service began to change to a new leadership model in response to controversies over resources (see Chapter 4 for a Pacific Northwest example). It was clear by the early 1990s that the organization had to change in response to changing public attitudes and desires. Their New Perspectives initiative (Salwasser 1999, Robertson 2004) engaged all levels of the large (about 50,000 employees) bureaucracy, as well as a large number of important "stakeholder" groups in a search for a new purpose and leadership approach. This was clearly a response to the perception that most of the problems the agency faced were "environmental." We now see that all problems faced by all organizations are becoming more "environmental" because of increasing human population, much greater and broader availability of information, and the universal assumption of involvement and "say so" caused by the rise of market capitalism and democracy. Everybody feels they should have influence on everything that affects their life. Business leaders say they must "earn the social license to operate." People increasingly assert their right to try to control events with their votes, and to vote in the marketplace with their money.

Essential leaders are people who can use organizations to seek solutions to such problems in this changing human context. A major burden of this leadership mode is to acknowledge that there are few permanent solutions to complex problems. The most it is realistic to hope for are progress and positive trends. Indeed, leaders often find their most important role in providing the continuity and focus over time to create progress.

The contrast between the old leadership model and the new, environment-based essential one is clear, even though all leadership examples lie on an evolutionary continuum from old to new. Old leadership depends on a relatively few, "special," strong individuals operating in relatively closed systems, with access to limited and closely held information. Many current leadership theories and approaches attempt to remedy the fairly obvious inefficiencies of this kind of leadership by making old leadership ideas and actions more palatable, rather than changing to a new way of doing leadership business. Leaders are to become more sensitive, flexible, "nurturing"; more people are to be consulted about decisions; sometimes decisions are to be made by consensus processes in which the leader acts as a facilitator.

New leadership is emerging, particularly (but not solely) in the environmental and natural resource areas, for three specific reasons. The communications revolution has broken

L eadership that shares power—personally and organi-zationally—is very different from leadership that amasses power and seeks to defend hierarchies of authority. Apart from supporting compassion, discovery, and independent action, sharing power includes diverse groups and individuals and helps to gain high levels of participation and commitment from them. . . . For people to generally participate in organizational affairs, including decision making, requires they have power. Without it they are either excluded or present only in name. Without the power to participate, they cannot offer their true ideas and concerns; they can only comply with directives and prevailing values and norms that sometimes are not their own."

Source: J. Crowfoot, 1993. "Academic Leadership." In J. Berry and J. Gordon, eds. *Environmental Leadership: Developing Effective Skills and Styles,* 235, 236. Washington, D.C., and Covelo, Calif.: Island Press.

the near-monopoly that leaders in the past had on information and its transfer. Everyone now has access to increasing amounts of information. In the face of this information flood, systems can't stay closed, and old command-and-control mechanisms break down. Leadership naturally gravitates to those who can synthesize information and turn it into knowledge useful in problem solving. Better communication means, importantly, that people far away can be part of a "local" movement, organization, or enterprise. Internet sites devoted to intensely local controversies draw comment from around the world. The ferment about confidentiality and access on the Internet is another symptom of this change. It is possible to be informed about and actively involved in distant environmental problems without leaving home. Thus the number of "stakeholders" in any problem can increase almost without bound through self-nomination. This can enormously complicate solutions and the leadership task of producing them, but can also make solutions more robust if a broader segment of humanity supports them.

There is a less-noticed and related insight and revolution particularly important to the management of natural resources. It is now clearly understood that local communities are an integral part of any attempt to manage forests, water, or other resources (Vogt 1997, Bruner et al. 2002). This need to include people who are not formally part of the enterprise, coupled with the need to manage across bound-

> **A**n important social trend is the 'great ease of unob-structed two-way and mass communication through exploding communications and information technology.' "
>
> *Source:* Leader Survey quote.

aries (as when a river flows from one political jurisdiction or ownership to another) takes the "command" directly out of leadership, and changes the idea of "control." Systems are opened in ways they haven't been before. This was learned quickly by first-world people attempting to establish forest preserves or management areas in third-world settings. Management didn't work unless local people were included (not "consulted" or "recognized" but included in goal setting and the implementation of plans) (Pearce 1999).

Increasingly, the need for professional and personal diversity to solve environmental (and other) problems is clear. Although "diversity" is a watchword of both those who strive to be politically correct and those who criticize political correctness, the importance of diversity in solving complex problems is quite apart from this debate. Complex problems

> **O**ne of the major barriers facing today's leaders is the "lack of the human dimension to nearly all resource and environmental problem-solving exercises. If humans are considered, they are usually an add-on or afterthought."
>
> *Source:* Leader Survey quote.

require diversity of thought to be solved; often differences in personal characteristics and background produce different views of the same problem. This makes gender, ethnic, geographic, cultural, and even political differences a positive force for problem definition and solution in the presence of effective (essential) leadership. Thus, we now almost invariably use diverse teams of people to solve real, complex problems. This means that the person on the team with the skills and characteristics that apply to the portion of the problem being addressed at a given time should lead for that time if they have the capacity to do so. Thus, any given member of the team will lead or follow, depending on the topic and problem segment being addressed. Diversity is also increasingly needed to provide credibility. The days when "men in suits" could issue solutions from sequestered locations are ending. Unless the group proposing the solution is at least somewhat similar in background and outlook to the group that is expected to accept and implement it, they are less and less likely to be taken seriously. To quote a top executive from a major biotechnology firm, "We want our employees to look and act like our customers" (Ted Crosbie, Monsanto Corp., pers. comm.). Thus, the creation and management of culturally diverse groups becomes an ever-more-important leadership skill.

New leadership realizes that society, technology, and communication have all changed in ways that make old leadership increasingly obsolete. The main reason for this is that complex problems and rapidly changing conditions require more leadership from everyone in an organization. The leadership skills that were appropriate to the few are now necessities for the many. Thus, new leadership requires that everyone in an organization or on a team be able to lead effectively when her turn comes. The turn will come when a given individual's discipline or experience is the most ap-

Today there are over a hundred disciplines in the Forest Service. Employees come from dramatically different backgrounds and represent a wide range of values and have much less loyalty to the organization or its leaders. Effective leadership must deal with this new population if it is to be viewed as capable of solving their problems or achieving their goals."

Source: J. Sirmon. 1993. "National Leadership." In J. Berry and J. Gordon, eds. *Environmental Leadership: Developing Effective Skills and Styles,* 183. Washington, D.C., and Covelo, Calif.: Island Press.

propriate to meet the challenge at hand. New leadership asks organizations to develop leadership skills in all their people, and asks professional education to begin this preparation.

The current state of leadership at the forefront is one of transition from the old toward recognition of the strong and pervasive influence of the "open market of ideas and votes." The trend toward increased democracy and market capitalism, coupled with vastly improved communication and access to knowledge, continues to make every employee, customer, and client into a "stakeholder." Until new, essential leadership is learned and practiced, old leadership will find itself increasingly at odds with this open market, and increasingly ineffective.

Parts of the scholarly framework underlying essential leadership are found in a variety of sources. One of the first sectors to recognize and document the emergence of a new leadership mode was the environmental movement (Snow 1992). The overreliance of early-stage environmental organizations on a single charismatic leader has often proved to be fatal or nearly so, and has hampered the development of their leadership capability generally.

Barriers and Bridges by Gunderson, Light, and Holling demonstrates through a wide-ranging array of environmental management cases that there are no simple, consistent, widely accepted answers to environmental problems, and that an adaptive, place-based approach, requiring broad yet fine-grained local leadership, is the only one likely to pay off.

Thinking Ecologically by Chertow and Esty demonstrates, again through widely diverse cases, that old country-level, top-down regulation is not the best, or even a viable, approach to modern problems.

Forests to Fight Poverty by Schmidt et al. shows that the problem of deforestation will yield only to much broader, better coordinated, country-based efforts that will require a complex set of leadership tasks.

Ecological Stewardship by Johnson et al., a relatively massive analysis of the attempts to implement ecosystem management on the lands of the Forest Service, shows conclusively that scarcity, not of actual goods but of means to satisfy proliferating demands and divergent values, is the central problem, and that integrated leadership is necessary to solve it.

Scientific advances have assumed a central role in the definition of ever-more-complex environmental problems. We can't fix the "ozone hole" if we don't know it is there. New knowledge often creates potential for conflicts over values, whether about global climate change or genetically modified organisms. Thus environmental leadership must contain a component of the creation and use of scientific information, and its transformation to useful knowledge.

In general, environmental activism is shifting from detecting error to mending systems. One good indicator of this is the rise of industrial ecology, which seeks to design industrial production methods that minimize negative environmental effects by linking processes and industries into closed material cycles. One way to visualize the leadership impact of this shift is to contrast an individual, swashbuckling, fear-inciting environmental lawyer with a team of engineers, scientists, and citizens. The latter obviously needs more, and more complicated, leadership.

Thus there is now a different leadership environment: one that has to cope with more science, more values, and more people, requiring more and different leadership roles and skills. We are entering the era of "everyone leads, everyone learns to lead." Simultaneously, we are beginning to lead through learning and through thinking and cooperation. Leadership through learning is nothing more than the recognition that knowledge of the task at hand is a central leadership skill. However, the ever-increasing use of science and science-based information as the foundation of credibility and innovation has created the need for leaders to understand the general processes of science and to have in-depth mastery of some area of knowledge. Leadership through thinking and cooperation (Webster 1993) is the application of discipline of logic and the skills that draw people together to solve puzzles and create opportunities. Increasingly, formal partnerships are needed to effectively confront environmental (and other) challenges (Gentry 1998). Monolithic organizations with command-and-control leadership structures are being replaced by flexible, time-bounded alliances. Thinking and cooperation are the currency of these alliances, and thus are central new leadership skills.

None of the evidence indicates that the new leadership is more or less "human centered" than the old leadership, nor is there any indication that new leadership results in a recession from authority and accountability. Old leadership properly practiced was human centered, exercised authority, and was accountable. So is new leadership. The difference lies in how these are accomplished.

Essentials

 Society, technology, and communication have all changed in ways that now make old leadership increasingly obsolete.

 New leadership no longer is characterized by a single, charismatic leader. Complex problems and rapidly changing conditions require more leadership from everyone in an organization.

 Political activism is shifting from detecting error to mending systems. Thus learning, thinking, and cooperation are essential skills of new leaders.

 New leaders need to cope with more science, values, and people, requiring more and different leadership roles and skills.

 In the Essential Leadership era, "everyone leads, everyone learns to lead."

Chapter 7

Installing Essential Leadership in Your Life and Organization

In this chapter we describe how to learn, and how to install in an organization, the principles we discuss in the preceding chapters. Each of the characteristics that environmental problems share shapes what has to be learned to practice effective environmental leadership.

Long solution times mean that very often the same individuals that define the problem are not there at the "end" for its resolution. Recall the Northwest Forest Plan example from Chapter 4. The lead organization, the USDA Forest Service, has had four chief executives in the ten years from the plan's inception to the present time. And, almost always, the end is really the beginning of another phase of problem solving. This means that information, methods, and people have to be linked by effective documentation and institutional memory, so that effectiveness is not lost when the baton is passed from leader to leader, or from problem to problem.

Complexity requires a team approach, and usually blends several kinds of technique and explanation. The Rocky Mountain National Park elk management example described in Chapter 5 required scientific and technical input from disciplines ranging from plant taxonomy to ungulate physiology to sociology and law. The need to talk across disciplines means that jargon has to be kept to a minimum. Clear language is the best weapon to use to conquer complexity. Complex problems require information and participation from many, but their solution relies on interpersonal skills. Adeptness at working easily with other people equals and perhaps transcends disciplinary skill in importance. No matter how elegant your message, it will be without impact if nobody listens to it.

The *emotion-charged atmosphere* in which most environmental problems are confronted and solved means that conflict avoidance and dispute resolution are continuing and high-priority leadership skills, often even within the team that is trying to solve the problem. All complex problems include an element of negotiation and compromise in their solution. The large and diverse set of participants in the Seventh American Forest Congress (Chapter 4) negotiated intensely to reach a high level of agreement on a number of forest principles. All those agreeing to the new principles admitted to some degree of compromise with respect to the views they held at the outset of the process (Bentley and Langbein 1996). Ty Tice (1993) presents a "conflict management staircase" that describes as steps the options and processes between capitulation and war possible with respect to any contentious issue. The essential leader knows the stairway and is adept at the practices the steps describe, particularly negotiation, mediation, and fact finding. A good leader also sees clearly the consequences of the most extreme steps, war or capitulation.

A *scattered science base* again requires a diversity of technologies and people, and these must be brought together within the values and political dimensions that dominate most environmental problems. These requirements/demands mean that integration is a key to problem solving. For example, the primary way that conflicts over forest use were solved in the past was through allocation: some land for parks, some land for timber production, some land for watershed protection, and so on. Now, increasing human populations and prior land allocations require that several purposes be met using the same portion of the forest. This in turn requires integrated, rather than single-purpose, solutions. The creation and management of disciplinarily integrated teams are thus central leadership skills.

Expecting surprises means that when the unexpected strikes, at worst new information is recognized and used, and at best a contingency plan exists that applies to the surprise. Surprises can be valuable if they make one think of something new and ultimately positive, as they often do. Essential leaders are determinedly proactive.

The two most important conclusions we have reached from our own experience are that leadership consists largely of learned skills, and that most of us (individuals and or-

Henry Webster, former Michigan State Forester and originator of the "absorber of uncertainty" quote, distilled these leadership notions from his leadership roles in state and regional resource management:

- Make your organization and its mission relate to and serve major societal needs with a long-term view. Don't see this role as merely a budget strategy.
- Understand the linkages between resource issues and the rest of society and the economy that supports it.
- Help your employees and colleagues appreciate the importance of their actions in relation to major societal needs and directions.
- State your goals clearly and simply, in two or three affirmative sentences.
- Make linkages with political and staff leaders and help them quietly and in response to *their* needs, not yours.
- Adopt an intellectual orientation that keeps you in touch with primary knowledge sources. "Intellectual leadership lasts better than other kinds."
- Take opportunities to broaden your professional role beyond your own organization and locale; participate in as well as know the "big picture."

• Share credit for success widely, and help others with projects without overwhelming them or taking credit for their innovations and accomplishments.

"These observations are far from constituting any sort of theory about leadership, but they may be helpful. A common thread in all these points is the importance of a clear, simple idea of what you are trying to accomplish, as well as considerable flexibility in pursuing that goal. This point can hardly be overemphasized, even though leadership must often take place in disorderly systems. For complex and often disorderly resources and political systems—such as forests in state and regional settings—the elements of knowledge and cooperation (as opposed to competition) often underlay activities that are reckoned to be successful."

Source: H. Webster. 1993. "Lessons from State and Regional Resource Management." In J. Berry and J. Gordon, eds. *Environmental Leadership: Developing Effective Skills and Styles,* 120–21. Washington, D.C., and Covelo, Calif.: Island Press.

ganizations) spend too little effort learning them. We also think, but cannot prove, that the most effective leaders are the result of a combination of hard work and circumstance, rather than being "born leaders." A long-term, successful leader of a state forestry organization who created positive change over two decades was asked if one can learn to lead. His answer was, "I know you can; I had to" (James Brown, pers. comm.). Most successful politicians acknowledge that they learned to lead "on the job."

Circumstances produce leadership opportunities. Some are fairly large and clearly labeled, as when you are suddenly made, say, a department head. Others are harder to recognize. If you have an opportunity to lead your colleagues to the solution of an important problem because of your knowledge of the processes of problem definition and solution, you will demonstrate your leadership potential and gain valuable leadership experience. Part of the hard work is striving to be good at a technical area of knowledge, whether it is how laws are made or how trees grow, or any of thousands of other mentally demanding professional pursuits. This will give you the substance to solve problems in your area of expertise when they arise. But another part of the hard work is consciously learning leadership.

Thus, we suggest below how each characteristic and principle can be acquired or improved, and suggest a metaphor for propagating leadership skills in an organization (see the leadership tree, Chapter 1). We also describe insights from our study of the successful environmental leaders we have known. These range from tips on how to deal with angry people to philosophical aphorisms, for example, "leaders are absorbers of uncertainty." Their common thread is that we have found them exceptionally useful ourselves.

In this chapter we reiterate and expand on six ingredients of environmental leadership we think most important. These originated from our study of the leaders who wrote chapters for our first leadership book. We include them here because we think they are still valid advice:

- Prepare to be a leader and a follower.
- Think frequently and positively about change.
- Strive to develop the capacity to think broadly and flexibly.
- Learn to listen effectively.
- Know and practice your values/ethics.
- Be a lifelong learner.

First, we suggest that everyone should prepare to be a leader and a follower. Knowing when to lead and when to follow, and being able to change quickly between those

modes, allows people to function effectively in complex organizations solving complex problems. To learn this, try to
classify projects and other situations that arise in your organization using the problem definition criteria from Chapter 4. Which of those you describe call for your technical
skills? Rehearse what you would do if you had principal responsibility for leading in their solution. Also, think what
you would do to be an effective follower with someone else
in the lead. How could you make your best contribution as
a team member? For this exercise, and for those suggested
below, keep a journal in which you record and analyze your
results.

The second point is often talked about but difficult to
do: that is, to think frequently and positively about change.
Change is the rule now, and perhaps always was. Being ready
with tools and concepts to meet and use change positively
may be the essence of sustainable development (Gordon
1991). An effective environmental leader needs to anticipate
change and be ready to meet it. Practice analyzing trends in
your field and in society at large, and think about what
changes they might bring to your organization. A director

of technology at a large corporation once told me that his job was to see where society was going and to be there to meet it with new ideas and products (H. Hirschy, former Director of Technology for the Kimberly-Clark Corporation, pers. comm.). This practice in looking ahead and drawing conclusions is a practical way to develop that supposedly elusive leadership quality, "vision." We describe formal vision construction processes, but it is a skill you can practice constantly at low cost.

Our third point is to strive to *develop and keep breadth and flexibility of thought.* Thinking effectively about several things at once seems to be a hallmark of environmental leaders. Jacques Barzun (2000) has said that relevance is a property of the mind, meaning that finding connections between seemingly disparate facts or ideas is a high intellectual skill. Because of the complexity of environmental problems it is also a practical skill of the first order. The essential leader should strive to find similarities among seemingly disparate facts and situations, rather than immediately declaring them not relevant. The best way to do this is to read broadly beyond your discipline. We find reading history to be particularly helpful in this respect. In this use, the purpose of reading history is not to discover the "truth" about the past, but to see the connections among events that others have seen. Reading accounts of the same battle by contemporary participants and politicians, and later accounts by professional historians, can quickly show how the same complex event can be viewed differently. A good mental exercise in a dull meeting is to find something about the meeting that connects directly to something you actually care about, and to describe the connection and what it might mean in detail.

Learning to listen effectively is the only path to working effectively with a wide variety of people. Listening is also the least-practiced communication skill (note the number of courses and workshops that focus on speaking, compared with the number focused on listening). One good technique to use is called "active listening." In this mode, you try to paraphrase accurately what you hear back to the person to whom you are listening. You can do this either aloud or mentally depending on the circumstance. If you haven't tried this you will find it difficult at first, and you may also find that previously, when you thought you were listening, you were just waiting for an opportunity to talk.

Good leaders *set an ethical example.* We said in *Environmental Leadership: Developing Effective Skills and Styles* that a strong ethical base is best expressed not through examination and excoriation of the conduct of others but by workaday actions that are not explicitly labeled as "ethically based" or "conscience driven." We think it is a good idea to make two lists. The first one is headed "things I will strive never to fail to do because they are right." The second is headed "things I will strive never to do because they are wrong." Of course there are many lists of this kind already in existence, ranging from the Ten Commandments to professional codes of ethics to the entire body of laws to which you are subject. Restating or adopting those will not necessarily help you learn who you are. The point here is to think carefully where your values lie. Your ethical core is the central fact of your leadership ability. Try to write down what you really believe.

Finally, good leaders *are lifelong learners.* The pace of

ack Ward Thomas, writing on professional ethics, paraphrased the Wildlife Society's Code of Ethics, and then said, "One simple but essential admonition seems to be missing from these codes. Tell the truth! Telling the truth is so basic to ethical behavior that it should be the unspoken foundation supporting all other statements governing professional conduct." He then points out that acceptance and respect for diversity is a key component of professional ethics. He says, "For example, there are many different philosophies among natural resource management professionals concerning how they relate to the natural world. Remember, there are no inherent rights or wrongs in these philosophical positions—they merely *are*. Some tend to be anthropocentric and take a utilitarian view of the land—that is, land exists for people and is to be managed to satisfy people's needs. . . . Others are mainly biocentric in their philosophy, . . . view humans as part of nature, and subscribe to the admonition . . . to be concerned with organic wholeness, and to love that and not man apart from that."

Source: J. Thomas. 1993. "Ethics for Leaders." In J. Berry and J. Gordon, eds. *Environmental Leadership: Developing Effective Skills and Styles,* 36, 37. Washington, D.C., and Covelo, Calif.: Island Press.

change in knowledge and institutions requires this. A commitment to career-long education allows leaders to reassess their strengths and weaknesses continually and to develop the knowledge and skills needed to successfully meet change. At least two kinds of learning are involved. First, formal education through additional degrees, short courses, the Internet, and various forms of tutoring are important. In the latter form, it is good to have someone you designate as your "leadership tutor," much in the manner that many have "personal trainers" for physical fitness purposes. This need not be the president of your company or your country. Rather, it is more likely a friend with whom you can talk without embarrassment about leadership. It is also a way to discuss and refine what you learn in the second but equally important informal component of lifelong learning. These are the activities you undertake to sharpen your leadership skills, such as those described immediately above. For many reasons most people find it difficult to think or talk about themselves as leaders. For example, most of us find it distasteful when someone refers to him- or herself as a leader.

So it is important to have at least one colleague and friend with whom you can discuss your progress in learning.

There are five steps that can be used to "install" new leadership in an organization, but the methods for realizing the steps and monitoring their effects will vary with the group and its objectives and characteristics. Some organizations seem to gravitate naturally to environmental leadership (usually small, focused, and "lean" units). Others find themselves moving toward environmental leadership and spend large amounts of energy resisting, only to "lose" in the end. Everyone in the group or organization:

- learns the conceptual difference between essential and old leadership;
- does a leadership inventory: leadership characteristics, values, and skills (these can be represented in individual and group "leadership trees," see Chapter 1);
- participates in a leadership group that sets goals and identifies which characteristics and skills each member sets as learning priorities after sharing leadership inventories (leadership groups are usually five to seven people who work together);
- shares leadership problems, insights, and progress with the group at regular intervals; and

- monitors his or her leadership progress (see the next section).

The most important action is to emphasize talking and learning about leadership. There is a tendency to see leadership as hierarchical structure alone, or "bossism," which emphasizes command and control without giving reasons for either the command or the control (Scott Adams has the most telling and artful description of this leadership mode in his "Dilbert" cartoon series). Environmental leadership does not imply organizational democracy of the kind that has foresters keeping books, or bookkeepers keeping the trees. Nor does it imply that everybody votes on every decision. Rather, it implies the reverse. If everyone can lead when the appropriate time comes, and everyone else knows it, and knows when it is appropriate for them to lead, decisions can be made in the most timely way and without extensive consultation (translation: lots of unnecessary meetings). If everyone has a common way to define and solve problems, communication is vastly improved. If people are continually communicating about leadership, then they are more likely to recognize the need for it and to value it in others. Environmental leadership becomes a path to improved leadership and to environmental improvement in the broadest sense. Both the intellectual and physical environment will improve. Also, emphasizing leadership skills means that the quality (of people and organizational products) is continually in the spotlight, and the drive to pursue quality is reinforced.

The decision to deliberately pursue a transition to essential leadership should not be taken lightly. That goal can't be successfully achieved by one person, or a few in an organization, even a small one. Every member of the organization has to understand what environmental leadership is and why it is being pursued. That takes time and effort, and usually outside help at the beginning. Usually it takes someone from outside the group to be an organizer and resource person as the process is started, and to come back periodically to check progress and answer questions. Also, results will come only after a fairly long and intense learning period, and the learning never stops. It is not a quick fix but rather must become an ingrained attitude.

An organization will know it has begun to make the transition to new leadership when:

- most or all members of the group take initiative when the opportunity arises;
- decisions are made and implemented easily;
- few complain about a lack of information or authority, all acknowledge responsibility;
- groups form and function easily and well;
- people generally worry about results and not "inputs";
- "paperwork" decreases, "handshake" agreements increase; and
- disagreements are dealt with quickly and professionally instead of slowly and personally.

Much more widely dispersed and used leadership skills will allow individuals to assume authority and accountability much more frequently and easily. Many more people will be leaders as *new* drives out *old;* "organization chart" leaders will increasingly become followers.

Participation in leadership will be broader because of the need to include "communities"; those who are not in a chain of command but nevertheless are integral to the solution of the problem. Solutions will be driven by broad coalitions of agreement. The principle will be "the significant many and the trivial few." New leaders will be good participants and good at attracting and facilitating participation, and will create and manage *coalitions of partial agreement* that are sufficient to define and solve the problems at hand.

Recognition of human diversity in the sense of race, gender, politics, culture, and regional considerations will be part of every new leadership organization because of the broad participation necessary and possible in democracies and through modern communications.

All involved in essential leadership (eventually everybody) will need to study and practice both leading and following, and learn how to rapidly and smoothly change roles as the needs of problem and the organization change.

The continual presence and acceleration of change will be a pervasive influence; new leaders will constantly strive to forecast, understand, and positively meet change. Breadth and flexibility will be the tools that new leadership will use to meet change and ensure participation.

Listening to others, in teams, communities, across boundaries will be central to flexibility, breadth, and creativity. All groups contain more ideas, by definition, than any single individual within them. Often, careful listening alone will lead to solutions.

The new leadership will use knowledge of their own ethical limits and core beliefs to anchor and balance their need for breadth, flexibility, and inclusiveness. "Know yourself" will be more important than "know your enemy." In many environmental situations, "culprit" and "victim" are the same. Think of regional air pollution caused by automobiles, as contrasted with point-source pollution from factories. Most of us use automobiles, so to understand and abate the pollution they cause, we must come to terms with our personal use of them.

Lifelong learning, to increase breadth and flexibility, to add and synthesize scientific and technical skills, and to better understand people and leadership, will be necessary to continue to meet change positively and to help spread leadership skills. Organizations will increasingly adopt and learn new leadership rather than wait for it to happen to them.

Essentials

 Long times to solutions, complexity, emotion-charged situations, a scattered science base, and innovation require documented institutional memory, team and interdisciplinary approaches, conflict resolution and compromise, and a proactive, positive state of mind.

 Know and practice the six ingredients of leadership.

 Commit to implementing the six steps necessary to install organizational leadership.

 Emphasize talking and learning about leadership and continually stress enhancing leadership skills throughout your organization.

 Successful problem solving will be driven by new leadership models of broad coalitions of agreement not old chain-of-command hierarchies.

 "Know thyself" is more important than "know thy enemy."

Chapter 8

Lessons from
Popular Leadership Books

 To many people associated with the environmental movement, effective opposition to business and industry exemplifies environmental leadership. Thus it will seem strange to some to look for leadership lessons in the business literature. For those who consider capitalist enterprise the major environmental problem, we offer two reasons to read this chapter anyway. First, if private enterprise is seen sometimes or always to be the opposition, the phrase "know your enemy" provides incentive. If, like us, you think that business and industry are not only the source of some environmental problems but also potentially the largest engines of environmental improvement, it becomes even more important to know how leadership is viewed from their perspective. There is probably also wisdom in taking good advice wherever it can be found, regardless of its perceived ideological purity. As H. L. Mencken said of the communists (who were proposing that a Baltimore public golf course be opened to African Americans fifty years ago), "the time to disagree with them is not when they are right."

In *Environmental Leadership: Developing Effective Skills and Styles* we focused on the unique aspects of environmental leadership as differentiated from more traditional military or business leadership models because we thought we saw a new, "environmental" kind of leadership emerging in environmental and natural resource organizations. Now, we see convergence. Business leadership literature stresses many of the characteristics of environmental leadership, and environmental and natural resource agencies are increasingly embracing business leadership styles and techniques. To illustrate this convergence, and to support and enrich our leadership views and experience, we have extracted leadership vignettes from currently popular books about business leadership and applied them in environmental context. We also take lessons from a leadership book by a politician who, following an extraordinary event, became widely recognized as an extraordinary leader: Rudolph Giuliani.

Louis V. Gerstner, Jr. (2002), *Who Says Elephants Can't Dance?*

Mr. Gerstner, former CEO of IBM, is credited with one of the great leadership accomplishments in the annals of private enterprise. During his tenure, the largest computer maker in the world was transformed from a stumbling giant, ready to be broken into pieces, into a modern service company. At least early in his tenure as CEO, his most widely reported statement was, "There's been a lot of speculation as to when I'm going to deliver a vision of IBM, and what I'd like to say to all of you is that the last thing IBM needs right now is a vision." He was criticized by industry analysts for this, and discusses their reactions and what he meant at some length. "I said we didn't need a vision *right now* because I had discovered in my first ninety days on the job that IBM had file drawers full of vision *statements*" (first italics his, the second ours). He went on, "However, what was also clear was that IBM was paralyzed, unable to act on any predictions, and there were no easy solutions to its problems. The IBM organization . . . would have loved to receive a bold recipe for success—the more sophisticated, the more complicated the recipe, the better everyone would have liked it" (71).

Gerstner's definition of "vision" that emerges is interesting, and understanding it is particularly appropriate to environmental problems and organizations. First of all, he had an exceptionally simple, clear vision for IBM, based on his analysis of the future of the computing industry. The company had to be better at serving customers and acting quickly to change with the times and trends in computing. It also had to stay whole to use its size to be a more effective competitor and regain market share. He had developed strategies based on these two straightforward notions, and spent the next few years successfully working them out. He therefore implemented the vision concept exactly as it should be used. A good vision is based on an accurate prediction of the future, the hardest part, and a clear idea of what the organization or enterprise needs to do to meet that future.

It is also instructive to try to see what Gerstner thought the "vision thing" was. He mentioned lots of "vision statements" in IBM's files. And that is clearly what they were: statements, not viable visions. A useful vision is constantly in action, and may not even be supported by a carefully crafted, consultant-blessed "statement." What is important is to describe a desirable and possible future and, above all, to implement a strategy to vigorously and continuously pursue it. One of the key abilities of an environmental leader is to cause others to see, embrace, and implement the vision. Gerstner also implies that visions (of the kind IBM didn't then need) are bold strategies for success, seen to be better for being complex and sophisticated. In a trivial sense, any vision is a strategy for success, but most effective visions are not "bold." The ancient saw about flying applies: There are bold pilots and old pilots, but no old, bold pilots. Visions are better for being striking, apt, clear, and many other adjectives, but boldness, in the sense of high risk taking for its own sake, is seldom a good attribute of visions or anything else.

Visions are also made worse by being complex and sophisticated, because these attributes, other things being equal, make them harder to communicate. Environmental problems, as we have said, are usually complex and long term. They seldom are solved by bold, short-term actions. But they often yield to robust, sustained pursuit of a relatively simple vision. At the beginning of the twentieth century, the founders of the Society for the Protection of New Hampshire Forests saw that the headwaters of several major rivers important to downstream New England were being damaged by deforestation. Their vision was to see those lands maintained in forest cover through public and private action. Now, a hundred years later, the White Mountain National Forest exists in the headwater watersheds, and the organization still pursues the vision effectively through the acquisition of forest properties and easements. Countless "bolder," more complex conservation schemes have come and gone with less or no impact over the same time period.

Gerstner also makes a clear case for urgency, particularly early in a leader's tenure. He says, "I learned that whatever hard or painful things you have to do, do them quickly and make sure everyone knows what you are doing and why. . . . Dithering and delay almost always compound a negative situation." One of the most valuable personal traits for leaders to cultivate, in our experience, is "do it now." But the most important part of Gerstner's statement is "make sure everyone knows what you are doing and why" (68). General Eisenhower, commenting on the quality of the American GI in the Second World War, said that you could get American soldiers to fight well, and indeed do about anything, if they knew what they were fighting for and why.

Gerstner's book is a fascinating and personal account of a major corporate leadership episode. It contains many insights, methods, and situations that will be familiar to leaders in quite different organizations. We commend it to all.

Jim Collins (2001), *Good to Great*

Collins, a former Stanford business school professor, co-authored a business bestseller, *Built to Last,* in the 1990s. *Good to Great* is the result of his research on why some "good" companies succeed in becoming outstanding and other similar ones don't. A number of the ideas that emerge from his study seem to us to be similar to things we have observed about environmental leadership. Most seem to apply to most organizations, not just large corporations.

One of the most compelling ideas Collins advances is the "hedgehog" concept. Its name comes from Isaiah Berlin's rendering of a Greek proverb: "The fox knows many things, but the hedgehog knows one big thing." Presumably, at least to the originators of the proverb, the hedgehog prevails in confrontation with the fox more often than not, because by rolling up into a prickly ball the fox's many and varied attempts are defeated. Collins found that leaders that developed a "hedgehog" idea and stuck to it, succeeded. To us, this is quite similar to our use of "vision." The effective vision is simple, robust, based on an accurate view of the future and an organization's capabilities, and is relentlessly implemented.

Collins also found that leaders who launch radical change requiring major and abrupt organizational redefinition and restructuring often don't succeed in bettering their company in the long run and often ruin it ("the flywheel and the doom loop," 22). This is sobering, because leaders are seen by many (including us) as, among other things, "change agents." We do believe that good leaders do (and must) take calculated risks and bring needed change. But the operational word is "calculated." Just above, we talked about the disadvantages of being "bold." Organizational change in the environmental mode takes the form of making painstaking estimates of the future and then testing strategies to both shape and accommodate the forecast. One of the most interesting ecological management ideas emerging from the late twentieth century is "adaptive management." In this approach, leaders use management activities to test ideas in rigorous ways (Bormann et al. 1994). Adaptive management requires calculated risk taking. Two or more approaches to solving the same problem are implemented so that the results can be unambiguously compared. The less effective path is discarded, and new comparisons emerge. Over time, this approach should result in continuous, robust improvement in operations and useful knowledge. In its simplest form, it requires only that the consequences of management or leadership decisions be monitored honestly. This is quite different from making an untested blueprint for radical change, and betting the future of the organization on it. We think no good leader relies entirely on a prior notion of what "plan" is best to effect change, even when change is clearly and badly needed. Rather, change is pursued by enlightened trial and error, in a diligent but steady pursuit of a new vision. Effective old visions are abandoned reluctantly if at all. For example, the Wilderness Society focused for decades on increasing the area of federally designated wilderness areas, and, judged by that criterion, was a resounding success. When it suddenly broadened vision to include a wider range of environmental concerns, organizational chaos ensued for a time, and it is not clear that it has recovered its former purposefulness and effectiveness to this day.

What Collins called "level 5 leadership" was the key to achieving "greatness" from "goodness." "Level 5 leaders channel their ego needs away from themselves and into the larger goal of building a great company. It's not that Level 5 leaders have no ego or self-interest. Indeed, they are incredibly ambitious—but their ambition is first and foremost for the institution, not themselves" (43). Collins also found that effective leaders avoid the "genius with followers" model, where all solutions and advances come from the leader. We find these observations very consistent with our own experience. First, environmental leaders should be able to spread their ego over the entire organization they lead. Each leader must feel good when the organization and others in it succeed, whether they are directly involved or not. One of the most destructive leadership traits is a tendency on the part of a leader to compete with or denigrate those being led. Similarly, we see that spreading leadership ability and responsibility throughout an organization not only is strengthening but a key to solving environmental problems. It is imperative that those with the appropriate technical and social skills lead in solving problems calling for those skills. The "genius with followers" model effectively keeps this from happening.

In business, but also in academia, government, and the nonprofit world, many of us spend most of our lives trying to make good organizations better. Because of this, and because of its carefully researched conclusions, we found Collins's book relevant to environmental as well as business leadership.

Gifford Pinchot and Ron Pellman (1999), *Intrapreneuring in Action*

"Innovation is more than creativity. It is the creation and *bringing into widespread use* of a new product, service, process, or system" (12). Pinchot (the grandson of the Gifford Pinchot who was the key figure in the establishment of the National Forests) and Pellman insist that "intrapreneuring," the process of deliberate innovation, is a necessary component of all organizations. They further claim that the process "never happens according to a plan." "Good intrapreneurs are like broken field runners: they change the plan on the fly as new information appears" (xi). Also, they insist that this elusive process can nevertheless be both learned and managed.

In this way, their experience is quite congruent with ours. We firmly believe that leadership is, or can be, a learned skill and that it should be learned and practiced by everyone in an organization. Jay Espy (1993), a nonprofit leader, thought that vision (for example) was a property of the organization, not just of its titular leader. He said, "To see beyond the horizon, one must have some advance information and possess reasonable powers of deduction. To obtain advance information, the leader must confer with those who have sailed closer to the horizon—those who may already have a clear vision of what the future holds" (205). He goes on to point out that field staff, not the front office people, may have the clearest view of the future because of their daily contact with clients and customers. If they understand the nature and role of vision in leadership through the study of leadership skills, the whole organization will benefit.

We also believe that good leaders, like good innovators, are opportunistic (broken field runners in football are a sports analogy; they respond quickly to a rapidly changing environment). To quote Jim Lyons (1993), "Leadership happens when the right person is in the right place at the right time and seizes the opportunity to do something good" (101). Lyons's illustration of this is instructive, and is an example of environmental legislative innovation, or "intrapreneuring." In 1990 the staff of the House and Senate Agriculture committees, coordinated and led by Lyons, took an administration tree planting initiative and expanded it to include a broad range of forest conservation activities (including conservation incentives for private forests, urban forests, and a new international forestry initiative in the Forest Service). This response to an opportunity to innovate created the first forestry title in the series of laws known as the Farm Bill, the key recurring piece of legislation about the U.S. land base, and initiated conservation programs still in effective existence.

Intrapreneuring in Action: A Handbook for Business Innovation and its predecessor, *Intrapreneuring,* contain much good advice about how to make organizations more agile and innovative. Our favorite piece of advice is to "Bet on People, not just Ideas" (89). Because innovation never goes according to plan, the authors argue, concentrating on making sure people get the planned results is wrong. Rather, they say, concentrate on building a team that can "fix things fast when they don't work as expected" (90). Particularly note that they say "when" not "if" things don't work.

Rudolph W. Giuliani (2002), *Leadership*

Rudy Giuliani combines his personal narrative of the September 11, 2001, terrorist attack on New York City with the views on leadership he held as the city's mayor. Giuliani's leadership knowledge was gained over a lifetime of public service, and is packaged in chapters with such diverse titles as "Prepare Relentlessly" and "Bribe Only Those Who Will Stay Bribed." We have chosen to include this book in our list for two reasons. First, the experiences it describes arise in public service, not the private, for-profit sector. Second, his advice is often similar to ours, but it arises from a vastly different context.

Giuliani's most-reported leadership activities were his communications with citizens of New York, the country, and the world (including a speech at the United Nations) in the aftermath of the 9/11 attack. He provided information, reassurance, perspective, empathy, and hope to a shocked, confused, and vengeful people, and he was probably essential in the continued functioning of a vast and fractious city. One of the chapters in his book is entitled "Develop and Communicate Strong Beliefs." Our view is that communication is one of the top skills composing effective environmental leadership. Giuliani says, "A leader must not only set direction, but communicate that direction. He usually cannot simply impose his will—and even if he could it's not the best way to lead. He must bring people aboard, excite them about his vision, and earn their support" (183–84). He goes on to say that he developed, by trial and error (literally by "trial" through his experience as a trial lawyer), a communication style in which he studied the subject, developed his position and argument, and, when it came time to address an audience, did it in "his own words" rather than using a prepared speech. In this way, he sees himself as explaining, giving reasons for, what has happened or what in his view should happen. This method also allows him to tailor the message to the immediate audience.

This "tailoring" is controversial. Shouldn't the "facts" speak for themselves? It would be nice if they did. But when environmental problems are addressed (9/11 was among many other things a gross and immediate environmental problem), their complexity, their long-term nature, their contentiousness, and their weak science base ensure that the facts rarely speak unequivocally or say the same things to different audiences. The best the leader can do is clearly state the world view ("strong beliefs") that underlies her interpretation of what happened or what should happen. Carol Rosenblum Perry (1993) describes the communication "dyad." "The need to communicate—from *communicare*, the Latin root meaning, literally, 'to make common'—stretches back tens of thousands of years to images of bulls, bison, and horses, to curious spray-painted outlines of human hands, decorating cave walls. The embedded messages are lost to us, but then they weren't meant for us. Unfortunately, the messages that *are* meant for us often are as cryptic as Ice Age cave art, and for good reason. They masquerade as communiques. The message senders seem to lack either the skills or, worse, the intent to communicate. Or they fail to recognize that, to be true to its root, communication takes two" (47). This need for the communicating leader to constantly think about those she wishes to communicate with, specifically, at the moment, on her feet, is probably the central and most difficult leadership skill. Good teachers and politicians especially tend to develop this trait, but all who would lead need it to some considerable degree. Mayor Giuliani had it in spades, despite, by most estimates, not being a particularly articulate speaker or charismatic personality. His exercise of this skill in the wake of 9/11 served his city, country, and world extremely well. And by his own admission, it was wholly a learned skill.

Books about leadership carry the explicit or implicit notion that leadership can be learned. If it is wholly innate, why have books about it? But can it really be? Many still believe that leaders are "born, not made." We think if you consider carefully the leadership examples in the books above, it will be hard for you to maintain that view. Striving to learn, particularly from their own mistakes and experience, seems to be more the hallmark of the leaders described than any set of innate characteristics.

Essentials

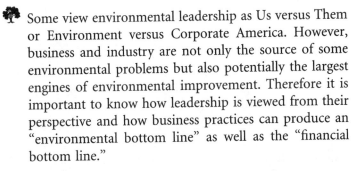 Some view environmental leadership as Us versus Them or Environment versus Corporate America. However, business and industry are not only the source of some environmental problems but also potentially the largest engines of environmental improvement. Therefore it is important to know how leadership is viewed from their perspective and how business practices can produce an "environmental bottom line" as well as the "financial bottom line."

Business leadership literature stresses many of the characteristics of environmental leadership, and environmental and natural resource agencies are increasingly moving toward business leadership styles and techniques.

IBM CEO Louis Gerstner's book *Who Says Elephants Can't Dance?* gives a somewhat contrary view of "vision" and why vision statements need to be simple, clear, robust (rather than bold), built on accurate predictions of the future, and implemented with sustained pursuit. He also emphasizes that leaders should do the most difficult, although painful, task first and when doing so, make sure everyone knows what is being done and why.

Often we talk about leaders as change agents. But in *Good to Great* Jim Collins illustrates why taking calculated risks rather than implementing radical change (again the "less bold" approach) is a more effective leadership approach. We believe this fits well with notions of "adaptive management" (explained by Bormann et al. 1994) and the necessity, in a complex and changing world, to test and adapt ideas and to pursue change with enlightened trial and error. Collins also encourages us to be "level 5 leaders." Level 5 leaders are ambitious, but they focus their ambition on the institution, not themselves.

Gifford Pinchot and Ron Pellman, in *Intrapreneuring in Action*, write about innovation ("the creation and *bringing into widespread use* of a new product, service, process, or system") and present it as a necessary component of all organizations. They further claim that the process "never happens according to a plan" and therefore people and building a team are the keys to success because when things don't happen as expected, the right people will be able to adjust and "fix things fast." Similar to our view that leadership is a learnable combination of skills and styles, Pinchot and Pellman believe that the process of innovation can and should be learned.

Perhaps no person in recent history has elevated his leadership stature as much as Giuliani following September 11, 2001. In his book *Leadership* Giuliani speaks to the power of communication and says, "A leader must not only set direction, but communicate that direction"

(183). Carol Rosenblum Perry advises that communication requires leaders to "make common" with their audience. We believe that communication and "making common" is nothing less than an essential skill needed for today's leaders. Facts, especially in highly emotional situations, are never as persuasive as effective communication of rationale, tailoring the message to your specific audience, and understanding that that communication is not just about the speaker and speaking.

Chapter 9

Essential Leadership Now and in the Future

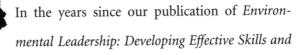 In the years since our publication of *Environmental Leadership: Developing Effective Skills and Styles*, we have confirmed many of our initial ideas and modified others. Today, although we feel that there are more similarities between environmental leadership and other kinds of leadership than ten years ago, we also believe there is a special distinctiveness about environmental leaders. After many years of surveying students and professionals about why they pursue a natural resource or environmental career, one constant theme emerges. They have a passion for natural resources and a desire to "do good" for the environment

and society. For most environmental professionals, their career is not about making money but about making a difference. This attitude and commitment make environmental work especially fun and rewarding.

We are, however, concerned about the future pool of natural resources professionals. Most natural resource programs have recently witnessed a decline in student enrollment. Environmental studies and sciences programs have increased in number and students, but they are still not clearly defined in terms of curriculum or career paths. The current situation is somewhat puzzling to us, because society today more than ever recognizes the importance of natural resources and the environment, and unlike years past, jobs are plentiful for graduates, although relatively poorly paid. Low initial salaries are probably a factor in determining the depth and quality of tomorrow's environmental leadership pool. The trend toward more educational requirements for entry-level jobs is another restricting factor. Increasingly a graduate degree, or more than one, is a characteristic of successful applicants for "leadership track" jobs in environmental and natural resources organizations, making the financial, time, and stress hurdles for entry higher. In the future, the "entry" degree for most jobs with a shot at the top will be a graduate professional degree and, in many, a doctorate. So, those who would prepare for environmental leadership positions should prepare now to invest the tuition and time in a graduate professional degree.

We continue to be convinced there is no one model of leadership. Skills and styles will depend on the problem and its context. We have, however, shifted some in our thinking about differences between what is thought of as traditional "command-and-control" leadership and the now more popularly accepted "participatory leadership." Unquestionably, as we have noted many times throughout this book, because of the complexity and strongly held values underpinning environmental problems, solutions must come from an inclusive process that invites all groups and interests to participate. This has resulted in exciting new techniques for collaboration and the emergence of diverse, longer-term partnerships and collaborative stewardship models. Participatory leadership, however, is often time consuming and heavy on process. It sometimes can lead to inertia or the inability to find sufficient common ground. Leaders need to have their eye on objectives and outcomes and know when it is time to take control of the process and "command"—that is, make a final decision among different alternatives and points of views. This level of decisiveness requires both personal and professional risk and can fall into the category of "politically incorrect." But good environmental leaders take calculated risks when the stakes are high enough, and must not be deterred by "inclusiveness" that becomes an excuse for indecision.

Gender was an important leadership issue ten years ago and continues to be so today. Many excellent books and articles now form a solid knowledge base that identifies and explains differences in male and female experiences, skills, and styles. Most conclude that these differences are consequences of gender-related social experiences that influence the way men and women perceive the world and themselves. Dissimilar life experiences lead to differences in communication and management styles, approaches to science, and ways of learning. Most often, these are stated as polar attributes. For instance, men are said to be more rational, competitive, goal oriented, outspoken, and hierarchical. Women are thought to be more intuitive, better listeners, more flexible, and more collaborative. For a time, we thought these differences might become less evident as more women entered the workforce and men took on additional family responsibilities. Nonetheless, we (along with 84 percent of the leaders we surveyed) still notice that gender-based leadership differences continue to exist. One of the noted differences is the observation that women are more people oriented. It seems to be true that women, compared with men, emphasize creating and valuing personal relationships. But our experience indicates that men will work well with a broad range of people if it results in the achievement of their own goals.

Another important difference is communication styles. When we participate in meetings, we often notice women not talking as much as men about their ideas or accomplishments. Women also show a tendency to ask questions rather than make direct statements. This could be interpreted as a leadership weakness in women's toolkit. But what it often reflects is a preference by some women to talk in smaller groups, or being brought up to believe it's just not polite to talk about oneself.

These are generalities, of course, and do not hold true for all men or women. We do believe, however, that in spite of the greater numbers of women in the workplace today, these differences will continue to exist, and will enrich the work environment for both men and women. Of most concern to us for both genders, but especially women, is the "push/pull" stress facing today's dual career families. Time and again we have heard young women professionals say that balance between work and home is most important to them. Identifying and mentoring the next generation of women leaders will require that those in charge help dual-career couples find meaningful careers in the same area, gain access to child care, and create an environment that fosters professional success without severely compromising personal and family values.

Some years ago we collaborated on an article with a title something like "Forestry and environment, from spare time to big time." The future of the environment and environmental leadership turns on making environmental matters "big time." If environmental leaders can make sound environmental policy and action mainstream political and economic realities to most people, companies, and legislatures, environmental causes will succeed and environmental goals will be met. If, however, environmental leaders cannot shed the "volunteer, crank cause" image environmental matters have inherited from the past, environmental issues will remain at the margins of society and the environment (and all of us) will suffer. Democracy and market capitalism are now the emerging reality of the world. Conservation and environmental activism have been the concern mostly of an often privileged but marginal segment of society in most countries. Now, or soon, everyone will have to be convinced that "environmentalism" is worthy of their votes and money.

Forty-five percent of our respondents thought environmental leadership was less evident today than in the past, and 71 percent thought it was more difficult today than in the past. We believe these responses reflect the increasing technical and political complexity of environmental problems and the broader, more contentious publics that have to be satisfied in their solution. Globalization, together with the availability of genetically modified organisms (GMOs), presents a good example of what we mean. Globalization of trade means that companies must compete for all markets appropriate to their products. Companies marketing agriculturally useful GMOs try to reach all markets, but the markets respond differently to the perceived environmental threats of GMOs. European consumers have reacted especially negatively to the prospect of "Frankenfoods." Other markets seem much less concerned, and seem to appreciate the perceived benefits of GMOs. Thus the solution to the environmental problems posed by GMOs will be different in different places, but the companies producing them and the agencies regulating them will be pressured to produce solutions that have universal reach. Therefore, environmental leadership may be less evident now simply because it is harder.

In spite of all the changes, good and troublesome, that have occurred in the recent past, we continue to believe that environmental leadership and leaders of the kind that we describe are critical to the future of human well-being worldwide. Therefore, there is no more urgent task than to encourage and nurture the next generation of environmental leaders. The most important message we have to offer is that environmental leadership consists largely of learned skills and styles and that learning needs to begin early and last a lifetime. This requires creating and tending to your own leadership tree, understanding the characteristics of environmental problems, knowing the elements of problem definition and solution, practicing the six ingredients of leadership, and installing organizational leadership. Following these steps, and with the desire for leadership, you will have all that is needed to be a leader. We hope you will enjoy the journey, and all the wonderful colleagues along the way, as we have.

Appendix

Leadership Survey Respondents' Organizations and
Positions at Time of Survey

William H. Banzhaf	Executive Vice President, Society of American Foresters
Edwin H. Barron	Associate Director, Forest Resource Development, Texas Forest Service
Charles W. Bingham	Retired Executive Vice President, Weyerhaeuser Company
Jean E. Thomson Black	Senior Editor Science and Medicine, Yale University Press
Bernard Bormann	Team Leader, Forest Service Pacific Northwest Research Station
Edgar Brannon	Director, Grey Towers National Historic Landmark, U.S. Forest Service
Alex R. Brash	Chief, Urban Park Service, New York City
Garry D. Brewer	Dean, University of California Berkeley Extension
Leslie Carothers	Vice President, Environment, Health, and Safety, United Technologies Corporation
Jared Cohon	President, Carnegie Mellon University
Mary J. Coulombe	Director, Timber Access and Supply, American Forest and Paper Association

Fred Cubbage	Head and Professor, Department of Forestry, North Carolina State University
William B. Ellis	Retired Chairman and CEO, Northwest Utilities
Elizabeth Estill	Regional Forester, Southern Region, U.S. Forest Service
Daniel Esty	Associate Dean and Professor, Yale School of Forestry and Environmental Studies
Charles H. W. Foster	Affiliate Faculty, Harvard University
Jim Furnish	Deputy Chief, National Forest System, U.S. Forest Service
Perry Hagenstein	Consultant, Natural Resources Economics and Policy
Mack L. Hogans	Senior Vice President Corporate Affairs, Weyerhaeuser Company
Jon M. Jensen	Senior Program Officer, The George Gund Foundation
Richard MacLean	President, Competitive Environment, Inc.
Denise Meridith	Arizona State Director, Bureau of Land Management
Gerald A. Rose	Director of Forestry, Minnesota Department of Natural Resources
Jeff Sirmon	Former Deputy Chief for International Programs, U.S. Forest Service
David R. Syre	Chairman and CEO, Trillium Corporation
Jack Ward Thomas	Professor, School of Forestry, University of Montana
Whitney Tilt	Director of Conservation, National Fish and Wildlife Foundation
Diana H. Wall	Director and Professor, Natural Resource Ecology Laboratory
Henry H. Webster	Research Associate Emeritus, University of Minnesota
George M. Woodwell	Founder and Director, The Woods Hole Research Center

References

Ackoff, R. I. 1962. *Scientific method.* Wiley, New York.

Barzun, Jacques. 2000. *From dawn to decadence: 500 years of Western cultural life, 1500 to the present.* New York: Harper Collins.

Bentley, William R., and William D. Langbein. 1996. *Seventh American Forest Congress Final Report.* New Haven: Office of the Seventh American Forest Congress (The Yale Forest Forum).

Berry, Joyce, et al. 1997. *Rocky Mountain National Park: Science-based assessment of vegetation management goals for elk winter range.* Fort Collins: Environment and Natural Resources Policy Institute, Colorado State University.

Bormann, Bernard T., et al. 1994. *Adaptive ecosystem management in the Pacific Northwest.* General Technical Report PNW-GTR-341. Portland, Ore.: USDA Forest Service.

Bruner, Ronald D., et al. 2002. *Finding common ground: Governance and natural resources in the American West.* New Haven: Yale University Press.

Carothers, L. 1993. Leadership in state agencies. In *Environmental leadership: Developing effective skills and styles,* ed. J. Gordon and J. Berry, 145–64. Washington, D.C., and Covelo, Calif.: Island Press.

Chertow, Marian R., and Daniel C. Esty, eds. 1997. *Thinking ecologically: The next generation of environmental policy.* New Haven: Yale University Press.

Collins, Jim. 2001. *Good to great: Why some companies make the leap . . . and others don't.* New York: Harper Business.

Crowfoot, James E. 1993. Academic leadership. In *Environmental leadership: Developing effective skills and styles,* ed. J. Gordon and J. Berry, 223–51. Washington, D.C., and Covelo, Calif.: Island Press.

Espy, James. 1993. Local voluntary organizations. In *Environmental leadership: Developing effective skills and styles,* ed. J. Gordon and J. Berry, 200–10. Washington, D.C., and Covelo, Calif.: Island Press.

Forest Ecosystem Management Assessment Team (FEMAT). 1993. *Forest ecosystem management: An ecological, economic, and social assessment.* Portland, Ore.: U.S. Department of Agriculture; U.S. Department of the Interior (and others).

Gentry, Bradford. 1998. *Private capital flows and the environment: Lessons from Latin America.* Cheltenham, U.K.: Edward Elgar.

Gerstner, Louis V., Jr. 2002. *Who says elephants can't dance? Inside IBM's historic turnaround.* New York: Harper Business.

Giuliani, Rudolph W., with Ken Kurson. 2002. *Leadership.* New York: Hyperion.

Gordon, J. C. 1991. Forestry and the environment: From spare time to big time. In *Agriculture and Natural Resources: Planning for Educational Priorities for the Twenty-first Century,* ed. W. G. Haney and D. R. Field, 79–88. Boulder, Colo.: Westview Press.

Gordon, John C., and Joyce K. Berry. 1993a. Environmental leadership: Who and Why? In *Environmental leadership: Developing effective skills and styles,* 3–12. Washington, D.C., and Covelo, Calif.: Island Press.

Gordon, John C., and Joyce K. Berry. 1993b. Six Insights. In *Environmental leadership: Developing effective skills and styles,* 270–74. Washington, D.C., and Covelo, Calif.: Island Press.

Gunderson, Lance H., Stephen S. Light, and C. S. Holling, eds. 1995. *Barriers and bridges to the renewal of ecosystems and institutions.* New York: Columbia University Press.

Johnson, K. N., J. F. Franklin, J. W. Thomas, J. C. Gordon. 1991. Alternatives for management of late successional forests of the Pacific Northwest. A Report to the U.S. House of Representatives, Committee on Agriculture, Subcommittee on Forests, Family Farms, and Energy, Committee on Merchant Marine & Fisheries, Subcommittee on Fish, Wildlife, Conservation and the Environment. Washington, D.C.

Johnson, Nels, et al. 1999. *Ecological stewardship: A common reference for ecosystem management,* vols. I–III. Oxford: Elsevier Science.

Lyons, James. 1993. Policy and legislation. In *Environmental leadership: Developing effective skills and styles,* ed. J. Gordon and J. Berry, 90–103. Washington, D.C., and Covelo, Calif.: Island Press.

McKibben, Bill. 1990. *The end of nature.* New York: Knopf.

Pearce, David. 1999. The economics of deforestation. In *Forests to fight poverty,* ed. R. Schmidt et al. New Haven: Yale University Press.

Perry, Carol Rosenblum. 1993. The environment of words: A communications primer for leaders. In *Environmental leadership: Developing effective skills and styles,* ed. J. Gordon and J. Berry, 46–66. Washington, D.C., and Covelo, Calif.: Island Press.

Pinchot, Gifford, and Ron Pellman. 1999. *Intrapreneuring in action: A handbook for business innovation.* San Francisco: Berrett-Koehler.

Robertson, F. Dale. 2004. *The history of new perspectives and ecosystem management.* General Technical Report SRS-74. Asheville, N.C.: USDA Forest Service.

Salwasser, H. 1999. Ecosystem management: A new perspective for national forests and grasslands. In *Ecosystem management: Adaptive strategies for natural resource organizations in the 21st century,* ed. J. Aley, W. R. Burch, B. Conover, and D. Field, 85–96. Philadelphia, Penn.: Taylor and Francis.

Schmidt, Ralph, Joyce K. Berry, and John C. Gordon, eds. 1999. *Forests to fight poverty.* New Haven: Yale University Press.

Sirmon, Jeff M. 1993. National Leadership. In *Environmental leadership: Developing effective skills and styles,* ed. J. Gordon and J. Berry, 165–84. Washington, D.C., and Covelo, Calif.: Island Press.

Snow, Donald. 1992. *Inside the environmental movement: Meeting the leadership challenge.* Washington, D.C., and Covelo, Calif.: Island Press.

Thomas, Jack Ward. 1993. Ethics for leaders. In *Environmental leadership: Developing effective skills and styles,* ed. J. Gordon and J. Berry, 31–45. Washington, D.C., and Covelo, Calif.: Island Press.

Tice, Ty. 1993. Managing conflict. In *Environmental leadership: Developing effective skills and styles,* ed. J. Gordon and J. Berry, 67–89. Washington, D.C., and Covelo, Calif.: Island Press.

Tuchmann, E. T., K. P. Connaughton, L. E. Freedman, C. B. Moriwaki. 1996. *The Northwest forest plan: A report to the President and Congress.* Portland, Ore.: U.S. Department of Agriculture, Forest Service, Pacific Northwest Research Station.

Vogt, K., et al. 1997. *Ecosystems: Balancing science with management.* New York: Springer.

Webster, Henry H. 1993. Lessons from state and regional resource management. In *Environmental leadership: Developing effective skills and styles,* ed. J. Gordon and J. Berry, 104–22. Washington, D.C., and Covelo, Calif.: Island Press.

Index